COLONIALISM
A Theoretical Overview

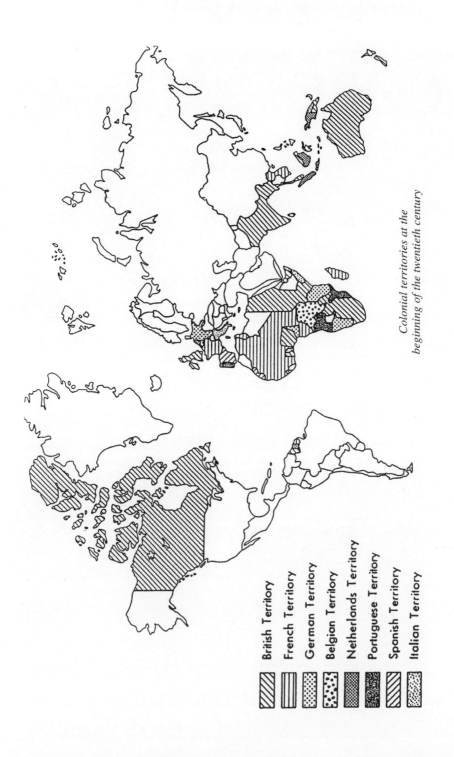

Colonial territories at the beginning of the twentieth century

British Territory

French Territory

German Territory

Belgian Territory

Netherlands Territory

Portuguese Territory

Spanish Territory

Italian Territory

COLONIALISM

A Theoretical Overview

Jürgen Osterhammel

Translated from German
by Shelley L. Frisch

 Markus Wiener Publishers
Princeton

 Ian Randle Publishers
Kingston

THE TRANSLATION OF THIS BOOK INTO ENGLISH WAS SUPPORTED
BY A GRANT FROM INTERNATIONES, BONN.

FOURTH PRINTING, 2002.

FOR INFORMATION WRITE TO: MARKUS WIENER PUBLISHERS
231 NASSAU STREET, PRINCETON, NJ 08542

BOOK DESIGN BY CHERYL MIRKIN
THIS BOOK HAS BEEN COMPOSED IN TIMES ROMAN BY CMF GRAPHIC DESIGN

LIBRARY OF CONGRESS CATALOGING-IN-PUBLICATION DATA
OSTERHAMMEL, JÜRGEN.
[KOLONIALISMUS. ENGLISH]
COLONIALISM: A THEORETICAL OVERVIEW/BY JÜRGEN OSTERHAMMEL;
TRANSLATED FROM GERMAN BY SHELLEY FRISCH.
TRANSLATION OF: KOLONIALISMUS.
INCLUDES BIBLIOGRAPHICAL REFERENCES AND INDEX.
ISBN 1-55876-129-2 HARDCOVER   ISBN 1-55876-130-6 PAPERBACK
1. COLONIES.   2. COLONIES—HISTORY.   I. TITLE.
JV51.08713   1996   325'.3—DC20   95-53736   CIP

FIRST PUBLISHED IN JAMAICA, 1997, BY IAN RANDLE PUBLISHERS
11 CUNNINGHAM AVENUE, BOX 686, KINGSTON 6
ISBN 976-8123-17-6
A CATALOGUE RECORD FOR THIS BOOK IS AVAILABLE
FROM THE NATIONAL LIBRARY OF JAMAICA

MARKUS WIENER PUBLISHERS BOOKS ARE PRINTED IN THE
UNITED STATES OF AMERICA ON ACID-FREE PAPER,
AND MEET THE GUIDELINES FOR PERMANENCE AND DURABILITY
OF THE COMMITTEE ON PRODUCTION GUIDELINES FOR BOOK
LONGEVITY OF THE COUNCIL ON LIBRARY RESOURCES.

Table of Contents

"Colonization" and "Colonies"

East India Company House, Calcutta, 1648–1726

These days, cultural critics and political polemicists often refer to a "colonization" of human life by bureaucracy and technology or a "colonization" of society by political parties. They typically associate this term with manipulation, usurpation, and illegitimate appropriation, terms that betray a negative assessment of everything related to "colonialism." It is the task of this book to construct a theoretical and historical overview of colonialism with a minimum of value judgments. In doing so, it will probe questions that have rarely been addressed in scholarly studies. These questions include the following: What characteristics of "colonialism" distinguish it from the many other types of dominance and processes of expansion evident throughout history? How can the concept be situated in relation to "colonization" and "colony," and to "imperialism" and "European expansion"? How can we grasp the particular nature of colonization and colony formation in the modern era?

In contrast to the ample research on "imperialism," there are few studies of the various notions of "colonialism" as they were understood in their time and today. No entry for this term is found in the seven-volume encyclopedia "Basic Historical Concepts."[1] There is nothing comparable to the "theories of imperialism" canonized in textbooks. The most insightful attempt at establishing a conceptual framework for colonialism comes not from a scholar of European overseas expansion, as one would expect, but from Sir Moses Finley, the historian of antiquity.[2] This expert on the foundation of ancient cities and empire building calls for a precise conceptual determination of colonialism specifically of the *modern* era. He considers it problematic to apply the concept to antiquity and the Middle Ages.[3]

Historians have shied away from attempts at terminological precision of the term "colonialism" because of its myriad facets. At one point or another between the years 1500 and 1920, most of the world's places and peoples came under at least nominal control of Europeans: all of America, all of Africa, nearly all of Oceania, and, if we include the Russian colonization of Siberia, the better part of the Asian continent. Colonial reality was multifaceted and often failed to conform to arrogant imperial strategies. It was shaped by particular local features overseas, by the intentions and opportunities of the individual colonial powers, and by broader tendencies in the international system. Colonialism must be seen from all of these angles, with a central focus on both perpetrators and victims. Even if we simplify the matter by following the conventional equation of colonialism and (European) colonial *politics* (one typical reference work calls colonialism "the politics of a state aimed at the acquisition and expansion of [overseas] possessions"[4]), the multiformity of colonial situations continues to confound efforts to define colonialism. Not only was the most comprehensive of all modern world empires, the British Empire, a patchwork quilt of ad hoc adaptations to particular circumstances. Even the French empire, which claimed to be organized according to principles of Cartesian rationality, was, in the words of Henri Brunschwig, the eminent historian of French colonialism, "in reality a colonial *system* [that] existed only on paper."[5] Colonization is thus a phenomenon of colossal vagueness.

Forms of Expansion in History

"Colonization" designates a *process* of territorial acquisition, "colony" a particular type of sociopolitical *organization*, and "colonialism" a *system* of domination. The basis of all three concepts is the notion of expansion of a society beyond its original habitat. These processes of expansion are a fundamental phenomenon of world history. They occur in six major forms.

1) *Total migration of entire populations and societies.* Large human collectives that have settled in one place and typically do not lead a mobile life as hunters or nomadic shepherds give up their original settlements without leaving parent societies behind. Expansion of this type generally entails military conquest, subjugation, and often suppression of peoples in the target regions. It can have several causes: overpopulation, ecological bottlenecks, pressures from expanding neighbors, ethnic or

religious persecution, enticement by rich centers of civilization, etc. This expansion type of the *exodus* occurred on every continent. It often led to new and precarious power structures in a world as yet unshaped by nation-building. This situation does not produce *colonies*, since no controlling center of expansion remains behind. Total migrations are rare in the history of the nineteenth and twentieth centuries. Deportations such as the *forced* resettlements of whole peoples under Stalinism in the early 1940s can be considered special cases. A relatively late example of a *voluntary* collective migration is the departure of the Cape Boers to the interior of South Africa on the Great Trek of the years 1836-1854, with the subsequent establishment of the two Boer communities of Orange Free State and Transvaal. This is of course not a *pure* case, since the majority of the Boers remained behind at the Cape without functioning as a controlling center for the Trek Boers.

2) *Mass individual migration*, the classic "emigration" in the broadest sense. Individuals, families, and small groups leave their home territories, motivated primarily by economic factors. They do not intend to return. In contrast to total migration, the societies from which they depart remain structurally intact. Individual migration generally takes place as a second-stage expansion process within established political and world economic structures. The emigrants do not create new colonies, but are integrated into existent multi-ethnic societies. Often they assemble in "colonies" in the figurative sense; the most highly developed form of these identity-affirming sociocultural enclaves is the American Chinatown. The degree to which these migrations are voluntary or forced is a variable within this type. Belonging to this category are not only the transatlantic emigration of Europeans to the New World and the other settlement colonies of the British Empire during the nineteenth and twentieth centuries, but also the *forced* migration of Africans to America resulting from slave trade, as well as the "coolie trade" with Chinese workers in the Pacific area and the settling of Indians in East and South Africa.

3) *Border colonization*. This term means *extensive* opening up of land for human use, pushing a "frontier" into the "wilderness" for agricultural purposes or to attain natural resources. This colonization requires settlement. Economically, it combines the mobile production factors of work and capital with natural resources tied to a specific place.[6] Only rarely is

the founding of colonies as separate political entities coupled with this type of colonization, since it usually takes place at the perimeter of existing settlement areas. One example is the gradual expansion of the Han Chinese agricultural zone at the cost of the pastoral economy of Inner Asia, particularly in the nineteenth and early twentieth centuries. However, this type of colonization can also proceed *secondarily* from new settlement cores overseas. The best known example is the development of the North American continent outward from its eastern coast. Industrial technology greatly increased the range of colonization as well as its ecologically destructive effects. Railroads in particular strengthened the role of the state (mainly in Eurasia) in a process usually organized by private groups. The most comprehensive railroad colonization under government sponsorship was the development of Asian Russia beginning in the late nineteenth century.[7]

4) *Overseas settlement colonization.* This special type of border colonization first appeared in the colonization movements of the Phoenicians and of Greek antiquity. It entailed the development of "settlement offshoots" across the sea in areas where relatively slight display of military power was required. Under early modern as well as ancient conditions, logistics made the decisive difference between this and true continental border colonization. The classic case was the initial phase of English settlement of North America. The founding groups of settlement colonies—"plantations" in the term of that epoch[8]—tried to build self-maintaining bridgeheads that were not vitally dependent on supplies from the mother country or on trade with the natives. The land was considered "rulerless," lacking legitimate political authority. The indigenous population was not subjugated and integrated into the colony in a subservient status, as in Spanish America, but instead was forcefully repulsed in the face of often violent resistance. The spheres of settlers and natives were separated both territorially and socially. In North America and later in Australia and elsewhere, the Europeans did not find efficient agricultural systems whose taxable surpluses could have supported a militarily based colonial apparatus—as did the Romans in Egypt, the British in India, and the Iberian powers in Central and South America. It was therefore not possible to divert an existing tribute flow from the coffers of the *ancien régime* to those of the new rulers. Moreover, the Native American population was

hardly suitable for forced labor in a European type of farming.

From these circumstances the first *"New England"* type of settlement colonies developed. This type entailed growth of an agrarian settlement populace that provided workers from its own ranks and by recruiting European "indentured servants." The intruders ruthlessly ousted the demographically weak indigenous population, considering it economically superfluous. In this manner, by 1750, socially and ethnically homogeneous regions of European settlement had been carved out in North America as cores of neo-European nation-building. Until that time, this situation had not existed anywhere else in the non-European world. Soon thereafter in Australia, the British followed this model of colonization under the peculiar conditions of an initial forced migration of prisoners. The British then proceeded to apply this model in New Zealand, in the face of violent resistance by the indigenous Maori.

A second type of overseas settlement colonization occurs when a politically dominant settler minority—usually with the help of the colonial state—expels an indigenous peasant population from the best land, but remains dependent on the labor of that same population and finds itself in sustained competition with it for parts of the remaining land. The settlers of this second type, which we can call *"African"* in light of its most significant modern examples (Algeria, Rhodesia, Kenya, and South Africa), differ from those of the "New England" type in their economic dependence on the indigenous population.[9] This fact also explains the instability of this kind of settlement. The European colonizations of North America, Australia, and New Zealand became irreversible, but in the African settlement colonies fierce struggles for decolonization erupted.

A third type of settlement colonization solves the problem of recruiting workers after the expulsion or destruction of the indigenous population by forced import of slaves and their employment in a plantation economy. We will refer to it as the *"Caribbean"* type, since this is where it most clearly occurred. There were less predominant instances in British North America as well. An important variable is the demographic proportion between the various social and ethnic groups. In the British Caribbean, blacks made up roughly 90% of the total population by 1770. During that same period of time, in the northern colonies of what was later the United States, blacks made up only 22% of the total population, and even in the later "southern states" no more than 40%.[10]

5) *Empire-building wars of conquest*, the classic or "Roman" form of establishing the rule of one people over another. An imperial center continues as the ultimate source of power and legitimacy, even if military expansion is fueled primarily by resources that are mobilized on the spot in the course of pushing forward. However, a centralized unified empire does not invariably continue to exist. The Arabic-Muslim expansion of the eighth century quickly led to a polycentricism of independent powers. The Mongolian world empire of Genghis Khan split into several successor states after two generations. Even the British Empire at its height consisted of three loosely connected spheres: the "white dominions," the "dependencies," and the "empire" of India, whose government could pursue its own subimperialist interests. As a rule, military empire building has come about not·by annexation of territory in "empty" areas, but by subjugating existing state and societal institutions. These institutions were adapted to the needs of the conquerors but not altogether destroyed in the process. A sudden and complete devastation of the previous system of rule, as was the case with the Spanish invasion of Mexico, was more the exception than the rule. In the modern history of expansion, conquest was often a protracted process that followed from initial contacts in which the Europeans were equal or even subordinate partners. Military conquerors behaved parasitically toward the dominated economy; besides securing order and facilitating foreign trade, the major function of the administration was to skim off tribute. Reorganization of tax levies regularly belonged to the first activities of a colonial power. Only in unusual cases, such as in parts of the Roman Empire, in Ireland, and in Algeria, did military conquest entail the establishment of settlers and large-scale land appropriations as well as the direct takeover of agricultural production by foreigners. The classic modern product of a military imperialism—British India—was never a settlement area. This type of expansion results in *colonial rule without colonization*, which we will classify as an exploitation colony. A very important variant is found in Spanish America. Despite a substantial influx of Europeans, the situation there differed greatly from that of colonies of the Indian type owing to the development of a creole population segment, which reproduced itself demographically. In contrast to North America, settlement colonization was not the main

purpose of colony building. Most of the immigrants settled in cities and never made up a majority of the population. By 1790, toward the end of the colonial period, first-generation immigrants and creoles of Spanish ancestry amounted to roughly one quarter of the population of Latin America.[11]

Expansion by wars of conquest led to varied forms of integration of subjugated territories into their respective empires, depending on the political traditions of the conquering power. Characteristic of pre-modern empires was the annexation of newly-won regions to the existing territorial government of the empire as provinces. Modern empires generally had separate colonial authorities in the metropolis to supervise administration on the periphery. It is important to note that this separation did not only apply to the European empires; the Manchurian Qing Dynasty (1644-1911) also had newly annexed territories in Inner Asia (Mongolia, Tibet, and Turkestan/Xinjiang) ruled by a special "barbarian office" (Lifanyuan). The American diplomat Paul Reinsch considers these special governing bodies the crucial characteristic of a "colony." According to Reinsch, a colony is "an outlying possession of a national state, the administration of which is carried on under a system distinct from, but subordinate to, the government of the national territory."[12]

6) *Construction of naval networks.* This form of *maritime* expansion involves the systematic construction of militarily protected trading factories. Expansion of this type did not normally lead to either inland colonization or to significant large-scale military annexation of territory. The extension of British power in India from Calcutta, Bombay, and Madras was atypical, at least before 1820. The chief purpose was to secure a trade hegemony, first in the case of the loosely linked maritime empire of the Republic of Genoa in the Mediterranean, then with the systematically designed and more tightly organized merchant empires of the Portuguese (Mozambique, Goa, Malacca, and Macao) and the Dutch (Batavia, Ceylon, and Nagasaki) in Asia. When the age of world politics began in the eighteenth century, the installation of naval bases gained a global strategic significance for Great Britain, the leading maritime power of the time, beyond the protection of trade interests. Naval bases (notably, Bermuda, Malta, Cyprus, Alexandria/Suez, Aden, Cape Town, and Gibraltar) and militarily significant "harbor colonies"[13] (Singapore, Hong Kong) were

among the longest-lived and most stubbornly defended components of
the British Empire. The military base was the only colony type that was
adaptable to modern circumstances on a long-term basis. It was able to
advance from the era of the gunboat to the era of the tactical air force.

Colonies: A Typology

The terms "colonization" and "colony" should not be too closely identified with one another, as we have seen in this attempt at typological
structuring. Colonization can take place without colony building, which
is the predominant form of frontier colonization. However, there is also
colony building that does not follow colonization, but originates in military conquest. This type of colony building is based on the sword rather
than the plow. Between both "true to type" pure cases is the "African"
type of settlement colonization, in which conquest created the condition
for large-scale settlement. The fact that settlers were also armed cannot be
overlooked, but at least in the early phases of colonization, the force they
used was not always authorized by a state.

A definition of "colony" that is valid for the modern era and takes these
issues into consideration must be narrow enough to exclude situations
such as temporary military occupation and the annexation of border areas
to modern national states. The rather juridical circuitousness of the following definition is the price of terminological precision.

* * * * *

> A *colony* is a new political organization created
> by invasion (conquest and/or settlement colo-
> nization) but built on pre-colonial conditions. Its
> alien rulers are in sustained dependence on a
> geographically remote "mother country" or
> imperial center, which claims exclusive rights of
> "possession" of the colony.

* * * * *

The following major types of colonies have arisen in recent centuries
as a result of the expansion of European nations, the United States, and
Japan:

1) *Exploitation Colonies*

- usually the result of military conquest, often after extended phases of contact without land claims
- purposes: economic exploitation (by means of trade monopolies, use of natural resources, and levying tribute rather than farming); strategic securing of imperial policies; national rise in prestige
- relatively insignificant numerical colonial presence, primarily in the form of civil bureaucrats, soldiers, and businessmen (not settlers) who return to their mother country after completing their assignments
- autocratic government by the mother country (governor system), sometimes with paternalistic solicitude for the native population
  Examples: British India, Indochina (French), Egypt (British), Togo (German), Philippines (American), Taiwan (Japanese)
  Variant: Spanish America, in which European immigration led to an urban mixed society with a dominating creole minority

2) *Maritime enclaves*
  - result of fleet actions
  - purposes: indirect commercial penetration of a hinterland and/or contribution to the logistics of a maritime deployment of force and informal control over formally autonomous states ("gunboat diplomacy")
    Examples: Malacca (Portuguese), Batavia (Dutch), Hong Kong, Singapore, Aden (all British), Shanghai (international)

3) *Settlement colonies*
  - result of militarily supported colonization processes
  - purposes: utilization of cheap land and labor, cultivation of forms of social, religious, and cultural life that are under pressure in the mother country
  - colonial presence, primarily in the form of permanently resident farmers and planters
  - early onset of self-government of the "white" colonists, disregarding the rights and interests of the indigenous population
    Variants:
    a) "New England" type: displacement and even annihilation of

the economically dispensable indigenous population; examples: the British New England colonies, Canada (French/ British), and Australia

b) "African" type: economic dependence on an indigenous labor force; examples: Algeria (French), Southern Rhodesia (British), and South Africa

c) "Caribbean" type: import of slaves; examples: Barbados (English), Jamaica (English), Saint Domingue (French), Virginia (English), Cuba (Spanish), Brazil (Portuguese).

II

"Colonialism" and "Colonial Empires"

Religious ceremony at Port Said at the opening of the Suez Canal

Colonialism: A Definition

How can "colonialism" be defined independently from "the colony"? The historian Philip Curtin speaks quite generally of "domination of people of another culture."[14] Although this formulation contains two decisive elements, namely *domination* and *cultural dissimilarity*, it needs to be made more precise. Not every domination by foreigners has been perceived by its subjects as *illegitimate* foreign domination. Between 1517 and 1798, Egypt, as a province of the Ottoman Empire, stood under the intrusive rule of the Turks, but this did not preclude general acceptance of the system by the indigenous Arabic-speaking populace.[15] The difference in language was compensated by a common belief in Islam and in the binding character of the Islamic notion of legitimate government.

To present in clear outline the particular historical nature of colonialism in recent centuries—perhaps we should say *modern* colonialism by this point—Curtin's basic formula must be supplemented by three additional components. First, colonialism is not just any relationship between masters and servants, but one in which an entire society is robbed of its historical line of development, *externally manipulated* and transformed according to the needs and interests of the colonial rulers. In practice, colonial governments scarcely attained such an ambitious goal, lacking the means to realize it, but this fact is of minor significance in the theoretical context of definition. Modern colonialism is based on the will to make "peripheral" societies subservient to the "metropolises."

Second, the kind of dissimilarity between colonizers and colonized is of crucial importance. Characteristic of modern colonialism, although not of world history as a whole, is the unwillingness of the new rulers to make cultural concessions to subjugated societies. European expansion has nowhere produced a "Hellenistic" cultural synthesis. Extensive acculturation to the values and customs of Europe was expected of the colonized. However, aside from certain exceptions mainly in the Portuguese empire, there was no significant counter-acculturation in which the colonizers borrowed on a large scale from the dominated civilizations. In the nineteenth century, the impossibility of such rapprochements was justified by the existence of allegedly insurmountable "racial" hierarchies. Any definition of colonialism must take into account this lack of willingness to assimilate on the part of the colonial rulers.

The third and final point is closely connected to the second. Modern colonialism is not only a relationship that can be described in structural terms, but also a particular *interpretation* of this relationship. The claim has even been made that it is principally an "ideological formation."[16] Ever since the Iberian and English colonial theorists of the sixteenth century, European expansion has been stylized grandiosely as the fulfillment of a universal mission: as a contribution to a divine plan for the salvation of the pagans, as a secular mandate to "civilize" the "barbarians" or "savages," as a "white man's burden" that he is privileged to carry, etc. These attitudes were always premised on a belief in European cultural superiority. American and Japanese colonialism also made full use of this kind of missionary rhetoric. Traditional cultures, such as the Chinese, proceeded on the assumption of the exemplary status and supremacy of their own civilization as if this were self-evident, without, however, imposing it on neighboring civilizations. Only in modern colonialism did this kind of ethnocentric arrogance take an aggressive expansionist turn, only here were the many bent by the few under a "spiritual yoke."[17] The colonialist structures of dependence can be characterized only incompletely without reference to the "spirit of colonialism" that animated them. This spirit has outlived the reality of the colonial era.

We have thus arrived at a definition:

* * * * *

Colonialism is a relationship of domination between an indigenous (or forcibly imported) majority and a minority of foreign invaders. The fundamental decisions affecting the lives of the colonized people are made and implemented by the colonial rulers in pursuit of interests that are often defined in a distant metropolis. Rejecting cultural compromises with the colonized population, the colonizers are convinced of their own superiority and of their ordained mandate to rule.

* * * * *

Now that we have defined "colonialism" independently of the term "colony," we must determine where these concepts converge. Colonies and colonialism normally go hand in hand. There are, however, borderline cases of non-congruence. *Colonies without colonialism* occurred in colonial societies without indigenous population majorities. Societies of this sort were homogeneously "white." They seemed to be replicas of European societies in "empty" land. This is especially true of the settlement colonies of the "New England" type. These colonies actively pursued frontier colonization, i.e., agrarian development of inland "wilderness," which destroyed the environments of native hunters and herdsmen. Because "native" subjects were lacking, however, they could not construct a system of domination, which is a basic component of colonialism. These societies were therefore not "decolonized" by stripping the power of the colonists and driving them out, as was the case in Algeria. They won their autonomy as national states as a result of abrupt revolutionary secession (as happened with the thirteen colonies, which then constituted the United States) or by gradual dissociation on basically good terms (Canada, Australia) from the European center of the empire.

At the opposite end of the spectrum we must consider the possibility of *colonialism without colonies*, situations in which dependencies of the "colonialist" type appear, not between a "mother country" and a geographically remote colony, but between dominant "centers" and dependent "peripheries" *within* national states or regionally integrated land empires. The theoretical construction "internal colonialism" was developed to categorize such cases, particularly the relationship between England and the "Celtic fringe" of the British Isles (Wales, Scotland, Ireland).

It can be argued that "informal colonialism" metaphorically strains the concept of colonialism.[18] Less problematic is the notion of *subcolonial* relations within hierarchically ordered colonial empires. The primary colonialist relationship in subcolonial situations is not between a colony and the metropolis, but between one colony and another colony of the empire. Examples include Angola, which at times was considered a sub-colony of Brazil, and the Philippine Islands, which in some respects were a dependency of Mexico. India was surrounded by a whole ring of satellites. The fact that there was no seizure of power by white settlers in the 1920s in the settlement colony of Kenya as there was in Southern Rhodesia is in no small measure due to the fact that the government of British India offered a protective hand to the Indian emigrant population in East Africa.

Colonial Empires and "Informal Empire"

Most colonies of recent centuries have been parts of colonial empires. The idea of empire assumes that *several* "peripheries" are subordinated to the empire's center in a star-shaped configuration. Generally they also have relations with one another, which are weaker than each of their ties to the center. In some cases the number of colonial possessions remains below the threshold that would justify our speaking of a colonial *empire*. Belgium controlled only two colonies: the Belgian Congo (Zaire) in the years 1885-1960 and Rwanda-Burundi in East Central Africa from1916 to 1962. The only territorial colonies of the United States were the Philippines (1898-1946) and Puerto Rico (1898-1952). The Spanish empire, which once spanned the globe, was reduced to a handful of miniature possessions in North Africa as the result first of the independence of the Latin American states, then of defeats in the Spanish-American War of 1898. Consequently, we can no longer speak of a Spanish "empire" in the twentieth century. In all of these cases we are dealing with *colonial possessions without a colonial empire*. Perhaps this is even true of the Dutch "empire," which, aside from Surinam, was limited to the Dutch East Indies (Indonesia) after the loss of Ceylon (1796) and the Cape of Good Hope (1794-1806). Of course, the Dutch East Indies, which had a large population, was of great economic importance for the mother country.

The overseas empires of the early modern era were by their very nature almost exclusively *colonial* empires. This situation shifted after the late eighteenth century with the increasing gap in economic productivity between the growth economies of Europe and the overseas world, the consolidation of world economic relations, the improvement of internationally available means of military intervention and the rise of political thinking on a global strategic scale. Great Britain, the leading economic and naval power between 1815 and 1880, could now pursue its economic and strategic interests with an array of options that reached beyond the acquisition of colonies. It was often sufficient to arrange for politically independent overseas states to open their markets to the products of British industry and to guarantee foreign property by law and in practice (as in the Latin American states, China, Japan, Thailand, Persia, the Ottoman Empire, etc.). This purpose was achieved by diplomatic pressure, military threats, and selective naval interventions, such as the "Opium War," which "opened" the Chinese empire in 1842. Colonial rule would have been too costly and would have involved unwanted political responsibility in all of these cases. Governing was left to more or less Anglophile indigenous rulers, who, however, were rarely enthusiastic "collaborators."

Differentiations between "formal" and "informal" securing of interests vis-à-vis militarily weaker and economically "backward" countries (in the parlance of the day), between "formal empire" and "informal empire"[19] apply not only to the British Empire, but also to the United States and Japan. Cuba, for example, a Spanish colony until 1898, was officially an independent republic between 1902 and Fidel Castro's takeover of power in 1959, yet almost its entire economy was in American hands, and the United States government intervened repeatedly in Cuban domestic policy. Cuba was thus a semi-sovereign region of exploitation for the United States, a classic case of "informal empire." The Japanese, on the other hand, supplemented their "formal empire," which consisted primarily of the immensely profitable colonies of Taiwan (1895-1945), Korea (1910-1945), and the puppet state of "Manchukuo" (the three northeastern provinces of China, 1931-1945, ruled de facto as a colony), by gradually widening their sphere of influence in China after 1905.[20] Before 1914, the Germans also built up an "informal empire" in China, Latin America, and the Ottoman Empire.

Let us recapitulate the three stages in securing interests used by "Big Brothers" toward "little brothers" in the nineteenth and twentieth centuries as follows:

1) *Colonial rule (formal empire)*: Indigenous rulers are replaced by foreign rulers (e.g., an Indian prince by a British governor). The pre-colonial political order ceases to exist or at least stops functioning freely. Representatives of the colonial power perform the central sovereign functions such as levying taxes, administering justice, and controlling police and military forces. All diplomatic relations of the colonized are taken over by the colonial power. In all other matters, the definitions of "colony" and "colonialism" we proposed earlier apply.

2) *Quasi-colonial control (informal empire)*: The weaker state remains intact as an independent polity with its own political system. It can conduct its own foreign policy and regulate routine domestic affairs. There is no colonial administration, but occasionally—especially in the area of finance—a mixture of foreign and indigenous administration (such as the Imperial Maritime Customs office in the Chinese empire). Nonetheless, the weaker state is only sovereign to a limited extent. "Big Brother" guarantees privileges for himself in "unequal treaties" as the result of selectively applied pressure ("gunboat diplomacy"). These privileges usually extend to the protection of foreign citizens from the enforcement of indigenous laws by means of consular juridisdiction and extraterritoriality, a well-defined free trade regime (low import duties when there is no customs sovereignty), and the right to station foreign troops on territorial waters and at prearranged points on land. "Big Brother" is represented by consuls, diplomats or "residents," all of whom intervene in domestic policy in an "advisory" capacity, particularly in conflicts over succession, and underscore their "advice" with the threat of military intervention where it appears warranted. In an extreme case, the indigenous office holders are powerless marionettes, but normally they possess considerable freedom of action. The ideal "collaborative elite," on which informal empires are invariably based, must have sufficient legitimacy and domestic authority to function effectively in the interests of "Big Brother." Informal empires are rarely motivated by strategy or prestige. Mostly they are a means to the end of securing significant economic interests (trade, direct investments, loans, etc.) that often came about *without* political support. Informal empire, unlike colonialism (formal empire), presupposes a distinct economic superiority of Big Brother. There must be a potential to "penetrate" an overseas economy. Again, unlike formal

empire, where colonial rule over one and the same territory is indivisible and exclusive, there can be several "Big Brothers" that concur on the principle of the "Open Door," that is, equal opportunity for all, or on the demarcation of national "spheres of influence."

3) *Non-colonial "determinant" influence*: There is neither a colonial system of domination between "Big Brother" and "little brother" nor are any special rights codified in "unequal treaties." Instead, the economic superiority of the stronger national partner or of its private enterprise (e.g., of multinational concerns) and/or its military protective function confers upon it opportunities to influence the politics of the weaker partner that its "normal" neighbors do not possess. This is a typical pattern of relations of international asymmetry in the post-colonial world.

Imperialism

The political and economic sphere of influence of the British and other empires of the nineteenth and twentieth centuries far exceeded their colonial core. In some parts of the world these empires exercised colonial rule, in others they made do with informal opportunities to control and secure their interests. At times they sought only to be a strong neighbor. The same results could usually be achieved in differing ways. From an *economic* point of view, it usually made little difference whether the foreign presence in an overseas land was a colony or a quasi-colonial, only nominally sovereign state that had to allow virtually unrestricted scope for foreign economic interests and itself had no say in vital domestic or foreign economic decisions.

"Imperialism" is the concept that comprises all forces and activities contributing to the construction and the maintenance of *transcolonial empires*. Imperialism presupposes the will and the ability of an imperial center to *define* as imperial its own national interests and enforce them worldwide in the anarchy of the international system. Imperialism thus implies not only *colonial* politics, but *international* politics for which colonies are not just ends in themselves, but also pawns in global power games. Typical "imperialist" ideas feature the use of colonies in compensatory deals between the Great Powers, which involve exchange, recognition of geopolitical claims on the part of third powers, and demands that

an alleged disequilibrium in the European balance of power be redressed. A "colonialist" attitude, by contrast, emphasizes the virtues of rightful acquisition, permanence, and responsibility and considers colonial subjects as "entrusted" to the care of the colonizers. Imperialism is planned and carried out by chanceries, foreign ministries, and ministries of war, colonialism by special colonial authorities and "men on the spot." The games of world politics in the age of empire must, however, always be seen against the backdrop of the development of a great power *system* and in the framework of slowly evolving structures of inequality in economic transactions across the globe.

"Imperialism" and "colonialism" are therefore not one and the same. "Imperialism" is in some respects a more comprehensive concept. "Colonialism" might appear to be one special manifestation of "imperialism," especially in the British Empire after 1780. However, because "imperialism" allows for a *worldwide* protection of interests and for capitalist penetration of large economic areas, one ought to be careful when employing the term to early modern colonial empires, which were not in a position to achieve these objectives. Only Great Britain and the United States have been imperialist powers in the full sense of the term, although the United States is a case of *imperialism without a major colonial empire*. France, Germany, Russia (or the Soviet Union) and Japan functioned as imperialists at various times in a more limited sense: either they did not attain a worldwide scale on a long-term basis or, like the Soviet Union at the height of its military strength, they were economically too weak to penetrate remote economies. *Colonial empires without imperialism* were the rule during the early modern phase of European expansion; only the seventeenth-century Netherlands could conceivably be excepted. In the nineteenth and twentieth centuries, however, the Netherlands became the prime example of colonial empires without imperialism. Between the World Wars, Holland was the third largest European colonial power after Great Britain and France. At the same time, it was scarcely an imperialist power, lacking as it did both international political ambitions and military might, and also lacking the economic option of being "informal" to any significant degree beyond its own colony Indonesia.[21]

III

Colonial Epochs [22]

Amsterdam receiving the tribute of four continents
(Fontispiece of *Historische Beschryvinghe
van Amsterdam*, 1663 by O. Dapper)

Problems in Mapping a History of Colonialism

Shortly after World War I, the French economist Arthur Girault determined that approximately one half of the mainland of the earth was covered with colonies. More than six hundred million people, about two fifths of the earth's population, stood under colonial rule: 400 million in Asia, 120 million in Africa, 60 million in Oceania, and14 million in America.[23]

No single linear historical process had led to this historical pinnacle of the expansion of colonial rule during the four centuries that had followed the Iberian annexation of territory in Central and South America. There is no history of colonialism *per se*, just histories of individual colonialisms. For a long time, scholarship only took the history of national colonial empires into account. However, for three reasons, this approach is tenable only to a limited extent. First, one need not endorse the theory of a consistent and precisely delineated evolution of a "modern world system" (Immanuel Wallerstein) to concede that there are certain parallels in the development of the colonial empires, even in their political evolution. For example, in the development of each colonial empire, the "hour of the bureaucrats" invariably arrives, the stage at which the conquerors, pirates, and settlement pioneers of the early phase are subdued or replaced and anarchic plundering is succeeded by regular administration and systematic economic exploitation. A certain "protection of the natives" forms part of this process wherever one is dependent on indigenous labor.

Second, the colonial empires of the early modern period were not hermetically sealed units. Ships' crews, colonial troops, and missionary societies were comprised many nationalities. The planter class that ruled the Caribbean sugar islands in the eighteenth century was pan-European by background and outlook.[24] As free trade spread through the colonial world in the course of the nineteenth century, business alliances ran across political lines. By 1914, substantial German capital had been invested in the British Empire, and Russian expansion was financed to a large extent by French investors. One of the most astute, moderately pro-colonial analysts of colonialism described this situation as follows: "Modern colonization is an affair of capital and not of men, and capital knows no country."[25]

Third and most significantly, viewing the situation from the vantage point of Madrid, Amsterdam or London overlooks the continuity of experience of the *colonized*, who often saw changes in their colonial masters. The Ceylonese dealt with first Portuguese, then Dutch, and ultimately British rulers; the Filipinos were ruled by the Spanish and then by the Americans. The constant was the *"colonial situation,"* the unchanging complex of rule, exploitation, and cultural conflict in ethnically hetero-geneous political structures that had been created by influence from with-out.[26] The background of the colonial rulers was of only secondary importance.

Non-Eurocentric historical scholarship therefore focuses on the rise and fall of particular societal forms—specifically of *colonial* societies—rather than on the colonial politics of European powers. The extent to which non-European regions have been influenced by colonialism at all is a matter of debate. Earlier historians assumed that the presence of for-eigners was the crucial factor in the history of a colonized country. The history of India in the nineteenth century has thus been written as the his-tory of British rule in India. For almost every other colony there are sim-ilar examples. The central theme of such accounts is the creation of order from chaos and of culture from nature by the energetic intervention of rational, well-meaning Europeans.[27] Early nationalist historical scholar-ship in the post-colonial countries of the "Third World," supported by neo-Marxist theoreticians, largely adopted this thesis of the omnipotence of the colonial rulers and simply attached an entirely different value judg-ment to it, holding a demonized colonialism responsible for all undesir-able developments. In a third phase, "southern" as well as some "northern" historians concurred that colonialism had largely remained marginal and was nothing but a footnote to the history of Asia, Africa, and America.

Such generalizations overstate the case, of course, but they raise the central question of agency in the history of colonialism. Recent specialized research has probed the choices and options of the colonized in particular colonial situations, often on the basis of indigenous sources that do not stem from colonial rulers. The Nigerian historian J.F. Ade Ajayi steers a sensible middle course between dramatization and trivialization of the effects of colonial rule: "Although the Europeans were generally masters of the colonial situation and had political sovereignty, they did not possess a monopoly of initiative during the colonial period."[28] We must therefore ask who held the historical *initiative*, as well as when and under what conditions. This approach throws into question the long-popular model of "impact and response," which held that the dynamic representatives of the "West" were those who acted, while the natives only had the option of *re*acting. In reality, the colonial situation is characterized by an ongoing struggle on the part of all concerned for opportunities to act. For the colonized this has also involved a struggle for human dignity.

Colony Formation: A Periodization

A rough temporal grid is an indispensable orientation to the variety of colonialisms and colonial situations over the past five centuries. Rarely has any historical phenomenon spread through the world more extensively and less uniformly. For good reason, most historians of European expansion have dispensed with the necessarily schematic means of explicit periodization. The less we rely on apparently significant data from reference works on the establishment and acquisition of colonies, the more complicated the task of periodization becomes. The data themselves are often historically incontrovertible. For example, it is well established that on July 14, 1884, the Imperial Commissioner, Dr. Gustav Nachtigal, proclaimed German "protective rule" over the Cameroon territory. But what do such data tell us? Let us consider a telling example of how data can be misleading. In the conventional view, Dutch colonialism in Indonesia began with the founding of the city of Batavia (Jakarta) in the year 1619, and French colonialism in Morocco commenced when France declared the country its protectorate in 1912. The two countries would thus appear to belong to very different epochs of colonial history.

The chronological distance shrinks, however, if we inquire into the origins of a *substantive* transformation of inland territories by exogenous political and economic forces. This date can be set at about 1830 for *both* Indonesia (more precisely, Java) and Morocco. In Morocco, the imperial seizure of power was the final step in a long process of informal penetration, whereas in Indonesia large areas remained virtually untouched by external influences a full two centuries following the arrival of the Dutch.[29]

The history of colonialisms is thus not only—perhaps not even chiefly—a history of conquest, acquisition, and flag-hoisting. It is a history of the gradual emergence of state structures and societal forms and their geographic expansion or contraction within nominally claimed regions. The densely populated and uniformly ruled modern nation-states of Europe had, at least in principle, a state power that was ubiquitous within the borders of a given country. By contrast, colonies were often marked by center-periphery structures. Mountains and forests, steppes and deserts evaded control by the center for an extended period of time or indefinitely, border wildernesses were difficult to "pacify," and wastelands were economically uninteresting to the colonial rulers. French colonialism had a different face in Algiers than in the Atlas Mountains; Spanish colonialism in Central Mexico differed from that in Yucatén. Within the empires, comparable dissimilarities could be found between important possessions and colonial hinterlands. There was a world of difference between a viceroy of India and a governor of British Honduras (Belize). In imperial backwaters, antique forms of colonialism that had long since been defunct in other places remained intact.

Many factors complicate periodization of the colonial experience: geographic diversity, the vastly differing types of non-European colonized cultures, the plurality of the colonial powers, and the distances and shifts between cores and margins.

The following discussion will highlight six periods that emerge from the continuity of expansion history of the last two centuries by virtue of their innovations in colony *formation*. The more comprehensive, non-colonial aspects of the development of the modern global system are roughly sketched as background.

1) *1520-1570: Construction of the Spanish Colonial System in Mexico*
Even before the Iberian conquests in America (the Aztec empire in
1521 and the Inca empire in 1533), some European overseas experiments
had anticipated elements of future territorial colonialism, notably the
Venetians in the eastern Mediterranean, the Portuguese on the Guinea
coast, and the Spanish on the Canary Islands. But not until the early
decades of the sixteenth century, as a result of circumstances that no one
could have anticipated, did a bifurcation of European expansion emerge,
resulting in what Adam Smith described in 1776 as a "project of trade" in
the Indian Ocean and a "project of conquest" in America.[30] Right from
the outset (about 1505), European trade in Asia was armed trade. Both the
Portuguese in the phase of their commercial supremacy and the Dutch,
who took their place in about 1620, intervened as merchant warriors in
existing Asiatic commercial networks. Of course, their domination of
these networks came about only gradually. From about 1740, the British
rose to become the most important European trading power in the eastern
seas. All three of these European powers established and defended forti-
fied coastal bases. Only in exceptional cases did territorial colonial rule
originate before the final third of the eighteenth century, namely on Ceylon, Western Java, and in the middle of the Philippine island of Luzon.
Over the course of more than two and one half centuries after Vasco da
Gama's voyage of discovery, there was no European colonial rule over
extended Asian territories.

European penetration in the Old and New Worlds had one thing in
common. In both hemispheres, advanced methods of bureaucratic organization were applied and refined. In the East, the East India Companies,
especially those of the Dutch and the English, became gigantic appara-
tuses, which at the height of their efficiency were among the most modern organizations in the world. In the West, the Spanish crown was faced
with unexpected challenges as a result of the rapid collapse of the Aztec
and Inca empires. "No European society until this moment had been
faced with an administrative task of such magnitude and such complex-
ity," concludes the Oxford historian John Elliott.[31] Conquests in Mexico
and Peru had been inspired by the knightly-feudal idea of the *reconquista*,
the battle against the Spanish Moors. However, there was no medieval
Iberian precedent for the establishment of a colonial administration,

which was essentially an instrument to tame the *conquistadores* and colonists. The result was a new kind of legal authority and a "form of government by paper, on a scale previously unknown in European history."[32] Without overrating the "rational" character of the Spanish colonial bureaucracy, at least after its heyday in the sixteenth century, we may still conclude that its creation was a notable organizational achievement. The characteristic features of the governance structures that originated before about 1570 lasted over two centuries.

2) *1630-1680: Establishment of the Caribbean Plantation Economy*

A second enduring innovation in sixteenth-century Ibero-America was the integration of colonized regions as export producers into intercontinental trade structures. Immanuel Wallerstein has demonstrated that long before Asia, America became the first overseas "periphery" of the "European world economy," that is, a dependent area to which the function of supplying primary goods was assigned.[33] Two decisive points are evident here. First, export-oriented production sectors were created *anew*. The Europeans did not merely "tap" previously existing sources of raw materials and finished products, as was typical in Asia. Second, forms of *unfree* labor were introduced or perfected for this purpose. Cases in point are Peruvian silver mining and, even more strikingly, sugar production in Portuguese Brazil.

After 1570, the plantation as a form of enterprise became widespread in Brazil. On the plantation, workers brought in from Africa as slaves produced goods for the European market. The expansion of the Dutch, English and French into the world of the Caribbean islands, which had first been dominated by Spain, was rooted in internal European rivalries for power, but was primarily motivated by the wish to imitate the road to success of the sugar economy.[34] The Dutch, who occupied a colony in Northern Brazil (Pernambuco) in 1637-1654, brought the "sugar revolution" from Brazil to the Antilles. Colonization in the Caribbean area also began with a "wild" phase. However, the piracy that first dominated the area was pushed back after the 1640s. One after the other, the larger islands got into the hands of the English (Barbados in 1627, Jamaica in 1655) or the French (Guadeloupe and Martinique in 1635, St. Domingue [the western part of the island of Hispaniola] in 1664). Only in Cuba did the Spanish prevail. Everywhere plantations were laid out; around 1680 the technical and social structures were established. By 1700 about 450,000 Africans had been transported by force to the non-Spanish Caribbean; simultaneously, 600,000 were brought to Brazil. In the eighteenth century, the British, French, and Dutch Caribbean islands became the largest slave importers in the world (about 3,300,000 people were brought to these islands).[35] Including British North America south of Virginia, colonial commodities produced by slaves dominated the world trade of the eighteenth century. Jamaica and St. Domingue were at that time easily the most profitable tropical possessions of their mother countries; St. Domingue alone appears to have produced more riches in 1780 than all of Latin America combined.[36] *Before* the mechanized factory system of the Industrial Revolution, the American slave plantation can be considered the most efficient form of large-scale commodity production, at the price of enormous human misery. At the same time, the colonial societies of the Caribbean, as traditionless and artificial new creations on depopulated land, were the most radical sociotechnical experiment of the age. Between the middle of the seventeenth and the end of the eighteenth centuries, the historical center of colonialism was located in the West Indies.

3) *1760-1830: Onset of European Territorial Rule in Asia*

These centuries were a period of unprecedented *global* power shifts and structural changes. In Spanish as in British America, stricter intervention on the part of the metropolises provoked successful endeavors for independence of the creole colonial elites. The creation of new nation-states did not, however, dramatically alter the mode of integration of these regions into the world economy. On the other hand, the slave revolution in St. Domingue, which in 1806 led to the founding of the black state of Haiti, as well as the gradual abolition of slave trade and slavery in the Atlantic region, ended the golden age of West Indian sugar interests. Unlike Spain and France, Great Britain could compensate for its colonial losses. It had become capable of worldwide military intervention even before industrialization by constructing a "fiscal military state."[37] The Seven Years' War, which can be considered the first "world war," had led to the collapse of the French position in Canada as well as in India. Napoleon's Egyptian expedition of 1798 certainly had jolting effects in the Muslim world, but did not result in the founding of a French empire in the Orient, which commenced in 1830 with the occupation of Algiers. Only Great Britain emerged with noteworthy territorial gain from the maritime race against France during the "second age of discovery." Australia was settled after 1788, initially as a penal colony. The conquest and settlement of New Zealand, which James Cook had claimed in the 1770s for the British crown, began in 1840.

The most important colonial advance of the period was the extension of the British position in *India*. The British East India Company (EIC) originally conducted trade from port cities. Later on, it became increasingly involved in Indian domestic politics, which were determined by the antagonisms of regional powers in the declining phase of the Mughal empire. Unlike the Spanish in Central America, the British in India at first pursued no plans to conquer and certainly no plans to proselytize. They were far from possessing military advantages over the Indian states until about the middle of the century. In Bengal, where British trade interests were increasingly concentrated, a mutually advantageous agreement was reached with the regional prince, the Nabob. Only when a collapse of this "collaboration" was brought about by a concatenation of causes did the idea of territorial rule originate. In 1755, Robert Clive, the future conqueror of Bengal, expressed a hitherto unthinkable idea: "We must indeed become the Nabobs ourselves."[38] From then on the British pursued a strategy of subjugation within a polycentric Indian state system, interrupted repeatedly by phases of deadlock and consolidation. Until the end of the colonial period in 1947, hundreds of seemingly autonomous principalities continued to exist, but after 1818 the British could consider themselves the "paramount power" on the subcontinent.

The East India Company continued to play its double role as business enterprise and state organization. Under constant supervision of the government in London it accompanied the military expansion of its sphere of power with the gradual establishment of colonial structures, which, in rough schematic terms, passed through a characteristic sequences of steps: 1) securing an effective trade monopoly, 2) securing military dominance and disarmament of any subjugated indigenous powers, 3) achieving a tax collection system, 4) stabilizing government by comprehensive legal regulations and the establishment of a bureaucratic administration, and 5) intervening in the indigenous society for purposes of social and humanitarian reform. This fifth stage was reached in the early 1830s. Not only did the age of European rule over highly civilized Asian societies begin in India, but India also became the prototype of an exploitation colony without settlers, a model for British expansion in other parts of Asia and Africa.

4) *1880-1900: A New Wave of Colony Formation in the Old World*

The period between 1830 and 1880 was certainly not a calm interlude in the history of European expansion. Only the Caribbean, once so rich, became a "forgotten derelict corner of the world."[39] In an age of "free trade imperialism," China, Japan, Siam (Thailand) and, to a greater extent than was previously the case, the Ottoman Empire as well as Egypt, now de facto independent from it, were forced to open their economies. Sovereignty limitations characteristic of "informal empires" were imposed on them.[40] Latin America, which was *no longer* colonial, and West Africa, which was rid of the slave trade but *not yet* colonized, were integrated into the world economy more closely than ever. On Java, the major island of the Netherlands East Indies, direct colonial intervention in the utilization of land began after 1830; the outer Indonesian islands were gradually subjugated in the period to follow. Foreign encroachment on continental Southeast Asia began after about 1820. First the lowlands near the coast fell into foreign hands: in 1852-1853 Lower Burma, and in 1857 Cochin China. By 1870, the later colonial borders could be distinguished clearly. During the entire period, the Tsarist Empire advanced in the Caucasus and Central Asia with military force, and shortly thereafter in the Far East with somewhat more diplomatic means, thereby intensifying the so-called "Great Game," a sustained cold war between the two Asiatic Great Powers Russia and Great Britain.

Despite these continuities of European world conquest and of ties between classic European diplomacy and "high imperialism," there is something to be said for marking a new epoch around 1870-1880. Most of the reasons can be found in the broader imperialist environment of colonialism, that is, in the structural changes of the world economy and international system. In terms of *colonial* history, the chief development over the last two decades of the nineteenth century was the European occupation of Africa, a singularly condensed expropriation of an entire continent termed the "partition of Africa." On the eve of this process, only South Africa and Algeria had been regions of European colonization, South Africa since 1652 and Algeria since 1830. Elsewhere the Portuguese (Angola, Mozambique), French (Senegal), and British (Sierra Leone, Lagos) made their presence felt in a more limited way. After all, by 1870 over 270,000 white people were already living in Algeria and about 245,000 in South Africa (including the two Boer Republics).[41] The further expansion of these early cores of colonization was also an impetus for the occupation of Africa in the last quarter of the century. The discovery of diamond deposits in 1867 and of gold in 1886 unleashed a development that changed South Africa into a capitalist center of growth and a magnet for international capital. At the same time, it strengthened white supremacy. In Algeria the same result was achieved simultaneously under almost purely agrarian conditions by extensive land transfers from the Arabs to a rapidly growing settlement population.

The actual "partition" of Africa in the years between the occupation of Tunis by the French in 1881 and of Egypt by the British in 1882 on the one hand and the Boer War of the years 1899-1902 on the other was initially a somewhat symbolic process. With treaties *amongst themselves,* the European Great Powers committed themselves to mutual recognition of colonies, protectorates, and spheres of influence. "Paper partition" was only slowly and incompletely transformed into effective occupation, "partition on the ground." However, the borders that were drawn endured with the later establishment of independent African national states.[42] For Africans, the so-called partition of their continent often meant the brutal disruption of bonds and established ways of life. However, partition could also result in the exact opposite: "a ruthless act of political amalgamation, whereby something of the order of ten thousand units was reduced to a mere forty."[43] Particularly in Islamic North Africa (Egypt, Morocco, Tunisia, and Algeria) as well as in parts of Asia (Vietnam, Korea, and Burma), colonialism encountered fairly complex proto-nation-states. Colonial rule in these countries was considered even less legitimate than elsewhere.

5) *1900-1930: Heyday of Colonial Export Economies*

Even though the "Age of Imperialism" was essentially over by 1914, the colonized peoples barely noticed this end of an era for some time. Only in Egypt was there a limited retreat of colonial power in the postwar period. At the same time, a new surge of colonization was taking place, putting the French (Syria, Lebanon) and the British (Palestine, Trans-Jordan, Iraq) in charge of the former Arab provinces of the Ottoman Empire. Not one of the erstwhile possessions of the German empire became independent; they merely switched colonial rulers. All of these developments took the legal form of "mandates" of the newly founded League of Nations and obliged the mandataries to be publicly accountable. By steadfast pedagogical influence on the still "immature" non-European peoples—"peoples not yet able to stand by themselves under the strenuous conditions of the modern world"[44]—a compassionate colonialism would at some undetermined point in the future be rendered superfluous.[45] The benevolent rhetoric of 1919, animated by the traditon of "liberal imperialism" of the prewar period, could not altogether veil colonial realities. The basic attitude of the Europeans and North Americans had scarcely changed. Nothing demonstrates this lack of change more convincingly than the fact that the "colored" Great Power Japan failed in its demand for the inclusion of a clause about racial equality in the covenant of the League of Nations.[46] Japan itself, of course, practiced a highly rigid colonialism in Taiwan, in Korea, and later in China. Its own colonialist ideology was not without racist overtones.

Especially consequential was the institution of mandates in the Middle East. Late Ottoman rule had weighed lightly on the peoples of the Levante and of the Tigris-Euphrates area, and was not always considered a foreign yoke. After World War I, the political elites of these countries saw no reason not to govern themselves. In Syria, for instance, an autonomous state was put into place in October 1918. It was terminated in July 1920 by the invasion of the French, who acted on the authority of the League of Nations. Since French and British in the Middle East, inspired by grandiose imperial fantasies, barely took note of regional aspirations and sensitivities and pursued their own interests with undisguised selfishness, they could never attain the legitimacy that the Turkish sultan had always possessed.[47] In the 1930s, the mandated territory of Palestine would emerge as the most explosive crisis spot in the British Empire, surpassing even India.

In the 1920s, the colonial world was more extensive than ever. As colonialism became extensive it also became *intensive*, beginning around the turn of the century in many areas and continuing beyond World War I. The colonial powers strove to make their administrations systematic, methodical, and even scientific. Excesses of violence were curbed. After a phase of bellicose imperialism, it was assumed that an epoch of tranquil enjoyment of the fruits of colonial rule would ensue. The notion that the colonial system might someday end was unimaginable to most politicians in the metropolises and the public, which was fed a steady diet of empire propaganda. The showy buildings and urban quarters that were now erected everywhere in the colonial world were conspicuously designed for eternity.

Infrastructural development of many colonial regions was pursued in this period. After the age of railroad construction came that of highways and the automobile, resulting in a change of the logistics of colonial control. Security forces could now be transported more quickly and flexibly to trouble spots. Moreover, the new technical avenues of "air policing" were improved and made more affordable; resistance movements could now be tracked down and attacked from the air.[48] Transportation by truck made remote areas accessible and at the same time created the basis for an indigenous transport enterprise.

Possibly the most consequential characteristic of the period between the partition of the world at the turn of the century and the onset of the Great Depression in 1929 was the growth of the colonial export economy.[49] New sectors were developed and existing enclaves of export production were expanded into the interior. European corporations of unprecedented size and power (e.g., Lever Brothers/Unilever) gained control of the lion's share of foreign trade. Some fields of business, such as copper mining in the Belgian Congo and petroleum production in Iraq, fell completely under the aegis of Big Business, just as the gold and diamond industries in South Africa already were. In Asia the type of tropical colonial society completely attuned to capitalist export production was developed most prominently in the British possessions Ceylon (Sri Lanka) and Malaya and on the island of Taiwan, which was ruled by the

Japanese. The Great Depression of the 1930s interrupted the export boom almost everywhere. It made formally ruled as well as informally controlled lands on the periphery painfully aware of the new degree of their external dependency.

6) 1945-1960: The "Second Colonial Occupation" of Africa

The period after World War II is no longer marked by colony formation, but by decolonization. It is appropriate to consider this period a *third* wave in the dismantling of empires.[50] The *first* decolonization was the national emancipation of most European possessions in the New World between 1776 and 1825. The *second* wave began in Canada in 1839 with the slow transformation of the settlement colonies of the "New England type," into de facto autonomous states. After 1907, they were generally known as "dominions" within the British Empire. The process received legislative sanction in the Statute of Westminster of 1931. Canada, Australia, and New Zealand became "as sovereign as they wished."[51]

The onset of the *third* phase of decolonization cannot be pinpointed. The endorsement of "home rule" in Ireland in 1922 may be regarded as the first major act of colonial liberation of the twentieth century. The emancipation of the "colored" world officially reached the historical agenda when, in 1933, the American Congress offered the prospect of independence to the Philippines after a ten-year transition period. While the Pacific War, started by Japan, delayed this timetable, on the whole it accelerated the end of colonial empires in Asia. Japan's own empire collapsed in 1945. Between 1946 and 1949, the League of Nations/UN mandates in the Near East were lifted, and the American, Dutch, and British colonies (other than Malaya and Singapore) in Asia won their independence. The nominal independence French Indochina attained in 1954, however, was just the prelude to a phase of renewed intervention that ended only with the defeat and withdrawal of the United States in 1975.

The decolonization of Africa began in Italian Libya in 1951. In 1956, the Suez crisis led to the collapse of the remaining military privileges and economic interests that the British had kept for themselves in Egypt. From that year until 1964, the larger part of Africa became independent. Portugal could maintain its colonies until 1974/1975. In Rhodesia/Zimbabwe the white settlers declared their independence from the British crown unilaterally; African majority rule was not attained until 1980.

In retrospect, decolonization may seem like a toppling of dominoes, an unstoppable process. It certainly did not seem that way to many contemporaries. The strategists of the British Empire recovered from the loss of the "Crown Jewel" of India with relative ease. At least initially, India retained close economic ties to the former colonial power after 1947. Until the Suez crisis of 1956, there was great hope for the consolidation of an informal empire in the Middle East. After that Africa, on which immense attention had been lavished since the 1940s, remained as an important imperial asset.

Never had Africa been of such paramount importance for the European powers as in the fifteen years following 1945, especially for Portugal, the oldest colonial power in Africa. France and Great Britain favored active developmental colonialism in sub-Saharan Africa including large-scale public investments. This developmental colonialism was to bring the metropolises direct benefits and the Africans the "maturity" necessary for a future independence. For British Africa there was even talk of a "second colonial occupation," an unprecedented extension of state functions down to the village level. Never had so many Africans come into such close contact with representatives of colonial power as in the very last years of the empire.[52] However, it was precisely this strenuous effort that contributed to the fall of the entire system. The promises of development awakened expectations in the Africans that could never be met, particularly since mounting economic troubles in the British Isles repeatedly provoked political decisions to the detriment of the colonies.[53]

IV

Conquest and Resistance

Uniformed African soldiers, commanded by white officers,
defeat poorly armed inland people in Tanganyika (Tanzenia).

(Excerpt of a drawing from the National Museum of Tanzania)

Colonial rule has virtually never resulted from sudden swift attacks on unsuspecting victims. Hernén Cortés' invasion of the Aztec empire was a major exception. Normally colonialism has come about gradually following "discovery" and and a period of initial contact. The geographer and historian Donald W. Meinig has distinguished a series of eight phases for America and, by extension, for the process of colonization as a whole: 1) reconnaissance of the unknown terrain, 2) gathering of coastal resources, 3) barter with the local population, 4) plunder and initial military actions in the interior, 5) securing of outposts, 6) imperial imposition (by symbolic assertion of claims to sovereignty and stationing a first group of official representatives, 7) implantation of a first group of non-military immigrants and initiation of a self-sustaining colony, and 8) development of a complete colonial ruling apparatus.[54]

Like every model, this one proves its value by allowing for historical deviations. Meinig's sequence applies best to Brazil, North America, parts of the Caribbean, and some of the South Sea Islands. For Asia and large portions of Africa it requires modification. Wherever Europeans faced armed and combative rulers, wherever their goals were limited to trade right from the start, and wherever climate and tropical diseases made settlement seem inadvisable, long periods of time passed between phases (6) and (7) or—in the case of the formation of exploitation colonies—in the direct transition from (6) to (8). Intermediate phases filled out these periods, during which the Europeans generally sought a peaceful *modus vivendi* with the local authorities, often formalized by treaties. Even if the first enclaves at the peripheries of the Asiatic empires came under the power of the Europeans by terrorist brigandage, as was the case with the Portuguese and the Dutch advance into the Indian Ocean, it was still necessary to reach accord with the host societies. In parts of Asia, the Europeans were directly dependent on tolerance by indigenous rulers. In 1662, at the height of their strength as a naval power, even the Dutch were driven from the island of Taiwan, not by the Chinese emperor, but by the regional warlord Zheng Chenggong (Koxinga). Taiwan remained uncolonized by non-Chinese until 1895.

Frontier Violence and Military Invasions

The establishment of both settlement colonies and exploitation colonies always involved the use of force. In the former case, there was an *ongoing* virulent relationship between armed colonists and the "natives" along the settlement frontier. Unchecked rule by violence prevailed in the interior of Brazil as well as on much of the North American frontier and for a brief period in Australia as well. In the permanent battle for the displacement of the "savages," every means, even genocide, seemed acceptable to the settlers and to paramilitary killer gangs, notably the Brazilian *bandeirantes*. The notoriety of the crimes of the Spanish conquistadors in the New World, perpetuated for centuries by the "black legend" of anti-Spanish propaganda, should not obscure the fact that the most violent form of European expansion was the settlement colonization of the "New England" type. Hunger for land coupled with indifference toward indigenous workers and other non-taxable native subjects, as well as a harsh theology of predestination and damnation that considered the Indians impossible to Christianize and civilize, combined to create an explosive propensity for violence. By and large, the Spanish view of colonization was, at least in theory, less inhumane than that of the English Puritans. Whereas the former focused on ruling over the residents of the country and utilizing the work force, the latter was intent on controlling the land, which allegedly required eliminating both weeds and "savages."[55]

The highly regulated power of the metropolitan states rather than the wild brutality of anarchic frontier fighters predominated as exploitation colonies grew. Here we can modify Meinig's model by identifying the following three phases: 1) initial contact or settlements, 2) conquest, and 3) consolidation. Concrete differences within such broad categories are considerable. The term "conquest" can have quite a wide range of meaning. Whereas the Aztec empire was overrun and destroyed, Spanish penetration into the neighboring Maya regions of Yucatén was more like slow infiltration. Large parts of sub-Saharan Africa were subjugated not by textbook cases of military campaigns, but by selective and sporadic use of force. The early German conquest in East Africa has even been described as "an extension of tribal war in which the Germans shared the plunder."[56] In other cases, for instance the great French expedition against Madagascar in 1895, a military "victory" was attained rapidly and affirmed by annexation, but a protracted guerrilla war ensued.

Colonial wars of conquest differed from warfare as practiced within Europe. Aside from limited interventions (such as those against Egypt in 1840 and against China in 1858-1860), colonial wars had a distinct goal of total victory followed by long-term subjugation of the conquered population and the establishment of enduring colonial peace. From a military point of view, these wars were no straightforward matter. Colonial wars were fought under less predictable conditions than wars within Europe. Nature was often more menacing than the enemy. Between 1793 and 1798, 15,000 British soldiers died of yellow fever and other tropical epidemics in Saint Domingue. In 1895, only twenty-five of the 18,000 French soldiers on active duty in Madagascar died at the hands of the Malagasies, but 5750 succumbed to malaria and other diseases.[57] Colonial wars were mostly "small wars" in the sense of "guerrilla wars" or forerunners of this type of warfare. The wars were also small because the available equipment and manpower were often quite limited. Large-scale, expensive campaigns like the British wars of conquest in India of 1798-1819, the various French expeditions in Algeria in 1830-1854, and Mussolini's invasion of Ethiopia in 1935-1936 were exceptions. However, "small" wars led to big burdens on the population that did not participate in the conflict. Especially in Africa, native porters were pressed into the service of the invaders by the umpteen thousands and worn out as anonymous human resources. Colonial troops, rounded up on the spot, often supplied the majority of the foot soldiers, resulting in self-conquest by Indians, Cameroonians, and many others. These troops had to be treated better than the conquered population in order to be useful. Each empire maintained colored elite troops that were called into action throughout the empire at crisis spots. Sikhs from the Punjab, Nepalese Gurkhas, and the King's African Rifles, the majority of whom came from the Sudan, are examples of these elite troops in the British Empire.

As social Darwinist thought came to prevail in the nineteenth century, colonial wars were viewed as wars to spread "civilization" to adversaries who were said to lack civilized rules of conduct. In a handbook published by the British war ministry, Sir Charles Callwell defined a colonial war as an expedition "against savages and semi-civilised races by disciplined soldiers."[58] Methods of warfare that in Europe were morally and legally barred were considered legitimate in the face of an enemy who did not seem to subscribe to the same cultural code. Even pacifists found themselves ready at times to justify this "other" type of war. Since almost no one in Asia and Africa thought in terms of a *purposeful* destruction of an entire populace (the originators of the German genocide of the Herero and Nama of South West Africa in 1904-1907 were an extreme exception), the argument seemed plausible that people were *forced* to engage in "savage wars of peace" (Rudyard Kipling) to free peace-loving savages and orientals from native despots and exploiters. This notion had at least a grain of truth, since the Europeans often were not invading tranquil idylls, but societies with a history of a high level of violence. The reproach that a group "lacked civilization" could of course be applied any number of ways. From the viewpoint of the Aztecs, for instance, who ritually slaughtered their Indian prisoners of war, the Spaniards of Cortés were fighting unfairly when they attacked sleeping villages, mistreated emissaries, and used hunger as a weapon.[59]

Defeat and Resistance

Europeans had to accept failure at times. The French in Algeria (1836), the British in Afghanistan (1842) and in the Sudan (1884-1885), and the Italians in Ethiopia (1896) all suffered defeat. National wars of liberation, the second type of war produced by colonialism, precipitated defeat in the twentieth century. As a rule, however, the conquerors attained their goals. There is no pat explanation for this typical outcome. If we were to judge by the 1898 battle of Omdurman, in which the British, equipped with automatic weapons, lost only forty-nine men, in stark contrast to the 11,000 Sudanese who perished, we might infer that the technical superiority of European weaponry was the crucial factor in conquest.[60] However, technical superiority was not always critical to success. A second explanation often advanced these days is the clever manipulation of native symbols in a cognitively immobile environment as effective ad hoc propaganda. This manipulation was practiced most notably by Hernén Cortés.[61] It would be misleading to generalize from this fascinating, albeit utterly Eurocentric notion. Few other non-European civilizations were as poorly prepared for foreign conquerors as the Aztecs, and only rarely did they cultivate extravagant notions like the oft-cited Aztec expectation of "white gods," an expectation that the Spaniards exploited. A stereotypical image of cultural paralysis on the part of the victims, who were said to freeze under the hynotic gaze of the imperial serpent, was more the exception than the rule. We need only think of the Maori in New Zealand, derided as "naked savages" by the Victorian English. The Maori cleverly repulsed an army that was far better equipped than its own during the years 1845 to 1869.[62]

Certain organizational *advantages* of the Europeans tended to tip the balance more than cultural *disadvantages* of peoples overseas. The Europeans benefitted from a compact and strictly goal-oriented rather than prestige-based military organization with clear commando structures, allowing for a quick replacement of commando posts without delay wherever necessary and a "Machiavellian" readiness and ability of the European political system to switch political alliances for tactical reasons once a shift in power structures had become evident.[63] In India, the way to military conquest was paved by the East India Company's diplomatic participation in indigenous politics.

Lack of unity among those facing colonization always facilitated conquest. Until people gained a feeling of solidarity with a group that extended beyond the confines of their own particular state, tribe or clan, disunity was more the rule than the exception. People in eighteenth-century India did not consider themselves "Indians"; people in nineteenth-century Africa rarely called themselves "Africans." Conversely, the Europeans were often perceived as merely one among many foreign groups in mobile societies. The highly threatening aspect of this newest type of foreigner was not immediately apparent. It is thus problematic to interpret "collaboration" and "resistance" as positions that can be assessed *on principal*, or even morally. Conduct in a given set of circumstances arose from the type of contact situation and the way it was interpreted.

In a justifiable effort to let the victims of colonial expansion come into their own as subjects of their history, recent research has dealt with "primary" resistance to colonial intervention in great detail.[64] In general, however, the military conquest itself was less likely to trigger major "traditionalist" resistance movements than *subsequent* encounters with repression, with demands of the colonial state for workers, soldiers, and taxes, and with the threat to the indigenous culture by missionaries. These resistance movements beset the colonial rulers unexpectedly, when "pacification" already appeared successful. The inevitable, usually brutal suppression of these movements often led to a reorientation of imperial politics. The revolt of the Sepoy troops in 1857, the so-called Indian Mutiny, marked a major turning point in British politics in and toward India. Even when the great primary resistance movements were no longer active, turbulence persisted in most colonies. Protest smoldered under the surface and erupted time and again on the local level. Since the colonial state had closed off many conventional avenues of flight and had thwarted resistance by the rural population, there often seemed to be no alternative to desperate confrontation.[65]

Colonial conquests realized their full potential only gradually. The consequences of these conquests were not immediately obvious. Even in Mexico, the classic case of a rapid collapse of a conquered state, it took the native Americans four or five decades to grasp the full effects of rigid colonial structures.[66] In India, roughly the same time span separated the late phase of conquest from the great Sepoy rebellion. Even though colonial rule provoked a social revolution in almost all regions in which it continued for a prolonged period, the potential for revolution was scarcely apparent just after conquest. Systematic interference in native societies was nearly impossible for initially understaffed administrations; they focused on establishing peace and a sound tax base. Royal or other state representatives were bent on taking in hand impatient conquistadors and "nabobs" greedy for booty. In doing so, they consciously fell back on pre-colonial arrangements. Thus, in Bengal in the 1790s, the traditional separation of trade and public functions was restored and the society was stabilized by a reorganization of the tax system. The end of the conquest phase, if it can be dated with any precision in a given case, also meant a *self*-pacification of the conquerors by overcoming their instincts for war and terror. The classically educated among them might have recalled the insight of the colonial governor Gnaeus Julius Agricola, active in Brittany between 77 and 84 A.D. His famous son-in-law Tacitus quoted him as declaring "that little was accomplished by force if injustice followed."[67]

The Colonial State

Colonel Prinz with his soldiers in German East-Africa
(German Foreign Office Archive)

Forms and Practice of Government

Colonial rule wore a variety of organizational guises. Not a single modern empire was administratively homogeneous. Despite its reputation for strict centralization, the imperial French Republic was an even more chaotic legal hodgepodge than the British Empire, which was well known for its piecemeal arrangements. At the beginning of the twentieth century, British colonial law distinguished more than forty categories of overseas territories, the control of which was distributed over three ministries: Colonial Office, India Office, and Foreign Office. In Rhodesia and inaccessible North Borneo (known today as Sabah, a constituent state of Malaysia) there was the institution of the private Chartered Company, already familiar from the early days of British expansion and privileged by the monarch. Bismarck also preferred this institution. The "crown colonies" were constitutionally subordinate to the colonial ministry represented by a governor. Examples are numerous Caribbean possessions, Hong Kong, the Falkland Islands, Sierra Leone, the Gold Coast (Ghana) and especially Ceylon, which in many respects was considered *the* tropical model colony. Kenya, Uganda, Somaliland, Nigeria, Njassaland (Malawi), Aden, and others were "protectorates." They were ruled more "indirectly" than the crown colonies (or, in the French empire, "colonies incorporées"), in which the colonial power had assumed complete sovereignty.

We should reserve the vague term "indirect rule" for three arrangements in which native rulers of demilitarized principalities or tribal regions were retained in positions of authority under the umbrella of supremacy of the colonial state. In the first of these arrangements, the approximately forty large and over 550 small "Princely States" of the Maharajas, Nizames, and numerous others were scattered throughout the territory of British India. These were areas of little economic interest for the colonial power. They were not permitted to manage their own foreign policy or even maintain any relations with one another. A permanent threat of intervention by the Indian Army hung over each of them. "Residents" in an "advisory" diplomatic role insured that a stabilizing politics of the domestic status quo be pursued at the courts.[68] A second, more direct variant of indirect rule allowed agents of the colonial power, aided by a small British staff and hiding behind a façade of dynastic rule in the old style, to have a say in everyday political matters in more than a mere advisory capacity.[69] This was the case in Malaya, Zanzibar, and Uganda, in parts of the Dutch East Indies, and in the French "protectorates" Annam, Cambodia, and Laos. In the third arrangement, in British tropical Africa in the 1920s and 1930s, indirect rule became a doctrine within an existing framework of direct colonial rule. Although it was seldom successfully practiced, its goal was to grant gradually expanding authority to chieftains and other "native authorities," who were to be shielded from the harmful influences of the modern world and to gain experience in local administration. The intention was partly humanitarian, partly utopian, but also conservative in the sense that by strengthening traditional authority, the wind would be taken out of the sails of the nationalist urban "agitators" who had just entered the fray. Until these aims were abandoned after 1942, indirect rule appeared to provide a safe non-nationalist basis for the political development of Africa.

Indirect rule was more a method of rule than an institution of constitutional law. The formal surface barely revealed the true power structure, as was evident in North East Africa. From 1899 on, the Sudan was jointly administered as a condominium of Great Britain and Egypt, but in reality it was altogether in British hands. Egypt was itself a cleverly concealed British possession, occupied in 1882 by British troops after a nationalist officers' revolt against the regime of the dynastic ruler, the khedive, cooperating with England and France. Originally, this "occupation" was to be a temporary measure, but it lasted de jure until 1922 and was not completely phased out until 1954. Under the singular fiction of a "veiled protectorate," Egypt was dominated by a British governor after 1883 behind the façade of an ongoing monarchy and an Egyptian cabinet. The governor's modest title, "consul general," was intended to obscure his almost limitless power out of consideration for the European Great Powers. As people said at the time, England ruled not Egypt, but the government of Egypt. Nevertheless, the Sultan in Constantinople was determined to consider all Egyptians his subjects.

Another, more clearly defined constitutional instance was India. Until 1858, the British-ruled parts of the subcontinent were under the nominal supervision not of the Crown, but of the time-honored East India Company, founded in the year 1600. Then they became an organizationally complex crown colony. In 1876, Queen Victoria had herself proclaimed "Empress of India," an act of more symbolic than practical significance and intended to stylize the British monarchs as the heirs of the Mughal emperors. Between 1858 and 1921, and thereafter to a more limited degree, all power was in the hands of the governor general (who was also the "viceroy"), "the supreme authority, in which was concentrated responsibility for every act of civil as well as military government throughout the whole area."[70] To maintain the status of the position, the governor general was appointed from the ranks of the aristocracy.

The forms of colonial constitutional law were of only indirect significance in everyday politics. They did not assume greater importance until the phase of decolonization. It cannot be assumed that a formally indirect system of rule was not intrusive. The case of Egypt illustrates this point most clearly. Life in a protectorate was not necessarily better than in a crown colony.

Going beyond the historical horizon of the British Empire, several basic sociological types of rule that corresponded roughly to the categories of colonial formation were concealed below the constitutional surface. Leaving aside the case of the neo-European settlement colonies of the "New England" type, which were early on provided with parliaments and then with responsible parliamentary governments, three forms remain: the minority settlement regime, the bureaucratic-patrimonial state, and the proconsular autocracy.

1) *The minority settlement regime* is characteristic for settlement colonies of both the "Caribbean" slaveholder type and the "African" farmer type. Before about 1830, there was an unchecked dictatorship of planters in Jamaica and the other British Caribbean islands. The enslaved majority and the middle stratum of freedmen were bereft of political

rights. Paris effectively controlled the ruling class in the French Antilles, but no such control came from London. A "plantocracy" enforced the laws it had designed, controlled the finances and the courts, and ignored the representatives of the king without censure.[71] Settlement regimes in Africa enjoyed unlimited latitude only when they broke away from the empire, as was the case in South Africa with the onset of the Great Trek in 1835 (and then a second time with the change of power of 1948 and the ensuing setup of the apartheid state, with all of its moral and cultural repercussions) as well as in (Southern) Rhodesia between 1965 and 1979. In Southern Rhodesia, home to a total of 63,000 Europeans in 1939,[72] politics had been conducted by British private citizens with minimal interference from London since 1889, the beginning of the British presence there. Their gains in political freedom—in 1923 the settlers had obtained "responsible government"—came with a substantially worse political and civil legal standing of the Africans than in the British crown colonies and protectorates. Even moderate constitutional concessions, as the colonial regime mitigated them in West Africa in its final years, failed to materialize. Quasi-autonomous, land-hungry settlers, not the government of the colonial state, here too proved to be the most vehement opponents of the native population, as is confirmed in Algeria. Under the Third and Fourth French Republics, neither Paris nor its governors intervened to counter the severe strategems of the settlers. Familial and other social ties, as well as political representation of "white" Algeria in the capital parliament, made North African settlers more firmly a part of their metropolitan system than the settlers in South Africa, Rhodesia, or Kenya. Safeguarded by the Algerian lobby in Paris (for which there was no British equivalent), the "colons" were able to strengthen a racist regime in Algeria that was highly disadvantageous to the Algerians, first legally, then politically and culturally. French civil rights were open to all Algerians—as long as they renounced Islam, a crime punishable by death according to Muslim law. Few chose this path. The French state never functioned as a "referee" between the population groups of Algeria, in contrast to the temporary practice of the British in Kenya and the South African Cape Colony.

2) *The bureaucratic-patrimonial state*. In the organization of its rule, Spanish America was a unique case in colonial history. A contrast with

the Portuguese and the early English overseas empires shows how inno-
vative the royalization of the early conquistador power and the structure
of a bureaucracy of civil servants were in the major colonial zones of the
Spanish empire. This bureaucracy was centralized, assertive, and in con-
formity with legal standardized rules.[73] Spain consequently intervened in
the society and culture of the peoples it subjugated with a vehemence that
later colonial powers rarely summoned up *intentionally* over extended
periods. Portugal, on the other hand, persisting in an older stage of state
formation in transition to the modern era, left the native authority structures in Asia largely intact.

Yet we must hesitate to call the Spanish crown administration in America the first fully modern colonial state apparatus. In any case, it was not
the immediate forebear of the colonial sovereign organizations of the
nineteenth and twentieth centuries, from which it differed in four
respects. First, it was unique to have the church fully subordinated to secular power for the purposes of colonial politics. The clergy apparently
became the most effective instrument of Spanish penetration of America.
Second, the system had been exposed to a gradual creolization since the
early seventeenth century and thus to an internal infiltration and external
delimitation by colonial Spanish, mostly urban oligarchies, which could
affirm the local interests of "settlers" in increasing opposition to the
imperialist viewpoints of Madrid. Never again did a colonial bureaucracy
with autonomous origins become the target of local forces in such a manner. Third, an increase in corruption resulted, which was structurally
inevitable given the contrast between the low pay of civil servants at all
ranks and the consumer demands of a society that linked social status and
conspicuous extravagance. A further issue, equally alien to modern
"rational" administrations, was the sale of offices. Selling offices was diametrically opposed to the meritorious principles of career and achievement. Fourth and last, despite the previously unprecedented centralization
of directives, the Spanish colonial system had an extremely complex system of checks and balances, division of powers of office, and supervision
by "councils" and other collegiate authorities. The Spanish colonial system was thus only superficially "absolutist." Its power, even at the top,
was highly fragmented.[74] Spanish colonial administration was, as a
whole, distinctly *early* modern.

3) *Proconsular autocracy*. No imperial ruling apparatus of the nineteenth and twentieth centuries experienced an *internal* dissolution comparable to the precarious Spanish administration. The state in the newer colonies was generally fully functional on the eve of decolonization. Even though the British in India had transferred many governmental duties to Indian corporations and opened the path to the parliamentarization of India after World War I, they proved capable of suppressing the mass uprising of the Quit India movement in 1942, the nadir of World War II. The political systems in most possessions of the modern colonial powers had a nearly omnipotent executive branch; of the European metropolises, only Russia still had this setup. The fact that power was often exercised "indirectly" and was partly delegated to native authorities, and that in some cases, such as Italian Libya, no strong state apparatus emerged,[75] does not alter the situation that rule was *essentially* unlimited by counterforces in the country itself. Power was concentrated in the office of governor. At the risk of invoking comparisons to Rome, we can therefore speak of "proconsular autocracy."[76] It is significant that rule was usually bound by law, even, at times, by constitutional law. Arbitrary despotism was rare.

Proconsular autocracy resulted from the crisis of early modern bureaucracy in the late eighteenth century, specifically from the crisis of two of its prevalent colonial manifestations, Spanish patrimonial administration and quasi-public Chartered Companies, which had now swelled into large organizations. This decisive phase of colonial state-building began simultaneously but without mutual influence in the two empires that were then the largest in the world. In Spanish America, the Bourbon reforms that peaked in the 1780s strengthened the executive branch, which had been undermined by corruption and was essentially the henchman of particular interests. At almost the same time, state influence on the East India Company expanded, and in 1786-1793 under governor general Lord Cornwallis the foundation was laid for modern Indian civil administration. In both instances, access to power was cut off from the established elites, respectively from the creole oligarchies and the Indians, to whom the new colonial bureaucracy remained inaccessible. This type of politics was enforceable in India, but not in America. The independent governments of Latin America carried on the line of the Bourbon state, where the latter had tightened its grip on the native population.[77] The "emancipation" of the Spanish colonies was just for white upper echelons.

Proconsular autocracy became the classic political form of exploitation colonies, following the model of British India. It was implemented in the British crown colonies and adopted in the tropical colonies of other powers, such as French Indochina and the Dutch East Indies. Even when portions of political power were delegated to native authorities in systems of "indirect rule," the state's monopoly on force and the autocratic framework as a whole remained unchanged. It is thus permissible to identify the "colonial state" in the narrow sense with proconsular autocracy.

Tasks and Administrative Structure of the Colonial State

The colonial state was no simple extension of the metropolitan political system to overseas possessions, but a political form in and of itself, even when the area under rule was declared an integral part of the national territory. This possibility was anticipated in the French constitution of 1791 and applied to Algeria in 1848. The liberal achievements of Europe did not usually extend to the colonized. Only in certain sectors of the "colored" British Empire were elected organs of representation installed under the banner of "dyarchy." Ministries accountable to parliament were added later. These organs of representation and ministries were granted designated areas of responsibility by the governor's office.

The colonial state had two main functions: to secure control over the subjugated peoples and to create a framework for the economic utilization of the colony. However much freedom of action a governor was granted by his ministry, the colonial state remained outwardly subordinate to the political authority of the mother country. Nevertheless, the colony was in practice "autocratic by nature."[78] An autocracy could embrace quite disparate manifestations of rulership, ranging from a mellow patriarchalism, as in German Samoa from 1900-1911 under Governor Wilhelm Solf and in the Philippines after the bloody war of conquest in 1902, to brutal regimes of violence like the Japanese reign in Korea. Usually the representatives of the colonial state valued their roles as strict "educators" of immature natives and as arbitrators over special interests.[79] Their roles thus contrasted with those of the settler groups that often formed in both settler and non-settler colonies. At least in theory, the administrations avoided becoming the instruments of individual interest groups. The French empire in the West African colonies retained a substantially greater leeway with the "colons" there than in the settlement colony of Algeria. The colonial state also tried to enforce its arbitrating role toward ethnic groups and social forces among the colonized. Often a politics of playing off ethnic groups or "tribes" against one another evolved, a tactic of "divide and conquer," which sometimes left a formidable legacy of ethnic rupture in its path.

As power at the grassroots of the political system dissipated, it became consolidated at the top. The colonial state made no de facto distinction between the executive and legislative branches and did not recognize an independent judicial branch. No matter what formalities may have been observed, it was a government by administrative decree of the governor, his council, and his staff. Often the district official was the representative of the colonial state. Because this district official was on the lowest rung of the administration, he came in daily contact with the subjects, and, as "King of the Bush," enjoyed nearly unlimited authority as tax collector, police chief, and even as judge. The colonial situation resembled the immediate aftermath of a victorious revolution, offering enormous leeway for political and social upheavals "from above."[80] Sixteenth-century Mexico was the clearest example. India was briefly a testing ground for adherents of the philosophical school of utilitarianism and certain doctrines of political economy. Colonial expansion appeared to open up new avenues for an "enlightened absolutism" of a sort scarcely possible in Europe by that time.

The principal traits of a colonial state are its dual character, subordinate and yet nearly omnipotent, its autocratic centralization of power at the top while using "divide and conquer" at the bottom, its self-perception as neutral authority over the parties, and, last but not least, the unbridgeable cultural gap between rulers and ruled. The fact that the fundamental loyalty of the colonial state lay *outside* its sphere of activity ultimately rendered it unstable or illegitimate, even if it strove for fair exercise of rule in particular cases. In the final analysis, the common good it claimed to represent was not that of the political structure over which it presided, but that of the empire. Decolonization thus implied nostrification of political rule.[81]

The primary task assigned to the colonial state by its founders was to guarantee law and order even beyond the period of conquest and "pacification" and after disarming the natives. Even though only few colonial systems were mercilessly repressive police regimes, the colonial state still reacted nervously and harshly to every stirring of opposition. Its guiding principle was never to let the initiative be snatched away and never to lose face. The state always had to have the last word; every provocation was to be punished with retaliation. The state suppressed not only openly anti-colonial protests, but also economically motivated strikes among the urban working class.[82] An astonishing number of colonial regimes were in a position to sustain this suppression until the very end of their existence. Comprehensive and professionally functioning colonial police forces were not in place until the 1930s. In Africa, they did not exist until 1950. The loyalty or disloyalty of the native police recruited for this purpose soon emerged as an important factor in the decolonization process. Trained security forces aware of their political role were among the legacies of the colonial powers to the successor states.[83]

Order may have prevailed, but it was not always accompanied by law. The question was *which* laws should be enforced. The colonial rulers were of course mistaken in their belief that they were venturing into areas that lacked a legal system. Indigenous law was not recognized as such, especially when it was not recorded. Often the "lawlessness" that the Europeans wanted to eliminate resulted from the breakdown of native mechanisms of legal regulation induced by the invasion itself. In other cases, especially in the Islamic area, deeply ingrained and resistant legal traditions were encountered. Although it is exceedingly difficult to generalize about colonial law, there was usually a striking "reluctance to accept jurisdiction over subject people."[84] This reluctance applied to civil law as well as to cases of criminal law that did not directly affect foreigners. The dissemination of European law was not a primary goal of European expansion, as was the spreading of Christian belief. The mother country and the colony remained two separate legal entities. A complete Europeanization of legal systems in the exploitation colonies was out of the question. The colonial state generally intervened in a regulatory capacity only in matters that did not directly affect its own interests, if it was forced to do so by missionaries or humanitarian activists, or if the incriminating practices radically contradicted European views. One example of the latter was the 1829-1830 prohibition of *sati*, the burning of widows in India. Most forms of slavery were suppressed, as well as polygamy, infanticide, child marriage, and so forth.

The split of colonial law into one set of laws for foreigners and another for natives sometimes led to a blatant double standard of justice according to race, especially in settlement colonies such as Algeria, where there was an especially harsh and demeaning "code de l'indigénat" for the Algerians. A double standard of justice was also found in exploitation colonies such as Japanese Taiwan.[85] In other cases, no special foreign law was imposed on the colonized; their own law was retained, often as an outgrowth of a romantic quest to codify and purify the "law of the people." In this process, native law was inevitably transformed, often beyond recognition. The result was a hybrid of native and European elements. Even more significant than the content of legal norms was the fact that the colonial state, in manipulating the law to protect its sovereignty, produced a judicial structuring of social relations unknown in pre-colonial times. This structure turned out to be irreversible even when colonialism ended.[86] A day in court now replaced traditional forms of conflict resolution. Court became an attractive option when a basic constitutional process was guaranteed, including due process and the right to appeal. The profession of law, which profited by litigation, became a means of social ascent and political awareness, especially in the British and French colonies. Growing familiarity with *procedural* equality under the law also nourished a demand for *substantial* equality. The partial Europeanization of the colonial legal system contained a potential for emancipation that extended beyond colonialism.

The bureaucratic intervention state

The colonial state did not hesitate to intercede even if the mother country held to a doctrine of minimal state intervention. It exercised comprehensive control over the colonial society in matters of legislation, legal judgments, law enforcement, and numerous other areas. Whenever its interest in a colony developed beyond trade and plunder and proceeded to a systematic exploitation of its resources, the colonial state had to pave the way for business interests with infrastructural projects (railroads, canals, streets, and telegraph networks), land development programs, customs and currency politics, and urban development initiatives.[87] The fact that there were often tensions with these interests need not concern us here. Rarely could the colonial state fulfill the many demands placed on it. Financial woes were a perpetual problem, since the metropolitan governments normally expected the colonies to support themselves fiscally. In some rare cases, private interests actually formed a state within a state and took administrative issues as well as the development of resources into their own hands. The best example may be the role of the Union Minière du Haut-Katanga, the copper corporation in the Belgian Congo since the 1920s. This role is usually labeled "paternalism."

In the early phases of conquest and "pacification," the colonial state often focused intensively on a small number of areas. Its immediate demands on the subjects in the form of taxes and labor service were especially high at this time. *Extensive* effectiveness came later, especially in the final period. In Africa, the colonial state evolved into an embryonic welfare state in the wake of the "second colonial occupation." In the earlier decades, a few colonial governments had already intervened more effectively in hunger crises than had pre-colonial rulers. The British Empire deliberated how it might raise the standard of living of its subjects following the poverty riots of 1937 in the Caribbean. The effects of these deliberations were evident chiefly in Africa after 1945. The late colonial intervention state was certainly a time of maximal manipulation. From the point of view of a substantial number of Africans, however, the so-called compassionate period[88] brought concrete advantages, especially improvements in educational opportunities and medical care. French and Belgian politics went furthest by introducing accident and health insurance, maternity benefits, family subsidies, and retirement pensions for their African labor elite.

The colonial state was bureaucratic in nature. One could even speculate that the advancement of bureaucratization in Europe received significant stimuli from the periphery. During the sixteenth century the Spanish form of rule in America displayed a far more complex degree of organization than that of the Iberian peninsula. In the British mother country, there was no bureaucratic apparatus until the structuring of the welfare state after 1945 that could have measured up to the administration of India, the Indian Civil Service (ICS), in both size and professionalism. The ICS was the model for all nineteenth and twentieth-century colonial bureaucracies. It was, moreover, the purest expression of the colonial state as proconsular autocracy and bureaucratic absolutism. Until the 1780s, during the "Nabob" period, India barely differentiated between government and private business. Afterwards began the gradual construction of a governmental administration, which, however, was not free of patronage for a long time to come. Not until the termination of the East India Company and the takeover of the government of India by the Crown in 1858 did the Indian Civil Service become a full-fledged modern efficient bureaucracy. The members of the ICS were recruited, by and large, from the ranks of the upper middle class of Great Britain after 1853 by competitive examinations among graduates of English public schools and universities (especially Oxford and Cambridge). They were to be "generalists." Mathematics, Greek, and Latin were the most important examination subjects. Once members of the ICS had been hired, they received training in jurisprudence and in Indic languages. The officials of the ICS, highly paid but barred from acquiring land in India, had a monopoly on all higher administrative positions; job rotation insured a fresh approach and precluded regional misuse of patronage. Only the chief of this executive hierarchy, the governor general, was appointed by the cabinet in London. ICS positions were among the most attractive and coveted posts that the British state had to assign. The ICS cultivated the esprit de corps of a highly competent aristocracy of merit, impartial to special interest groups and committed to the ideal of the gentleman. The Indian Republic continued the ICS as the Indian Administrative Service.

In Africa, the Belgians and French rather than the British recruited their higher colonial personnel by examination. In contrast to their British colleagues, trainees prepared for their duties in colonial academies. The Belgian administrators enjoyed the best reputation in Africa; the often incompetent and corrupt Portuguese administrators had the worst reputation.[89] The colonial administrations also differed in their willingness to admit natives. Obviously large numbers of natives were employed in menial and local tasks: on the railroads, in the postal and telegraph service, as secretaries, interpreters, messengers, and in the police and the military.

Access to bureaucratic elite posts was crucial. In sub-Saharan Africa, it was extremely limited, even in the French and Portuguese possessions, where no legal color bar existed. The Indian Civil Service, in which there had never been an *official* color bar, increased its percentage of Indians on staff after about 1919. In 1939, approximate parity had been reached: 589 Indian top officials compared with 599 Europeans.[90] A high degree of absorption of loyal native functionaries into the colonial state was of particular political significance in countries that lacked representative parliaments until the final colonial period (which was not the case in India, Ceylon, and Burma). In the British territories in Malaya, for example, a gradual indigenization of the lower administration began in about 1910, resulting in the development of a new class of declassed aristocrats and social climbers. This new class maintained close ties to the old elite but also to the colonial power.[91] A similar development was evident in the Dutch East Indies and in the Philippines.

Indigenous Collaboration

In the mid-1930s, the Japanese empire employed 52,000 Japanese civil servants to supervise twenty-two million Koreans.[92] At about the same time, there were 12,000 British in all ranks of the civil public service—from the governor to the railroad engineer—in all of India, a land of about 340 million residents (including the principalities).[93] The ratio in India was thus 1:28,000; in Korea, it was 1:420. India more closely approximated the average. In French West Africa, the ratio was 1:27,000, in Nigeria as high as 1:54,000.[94] The rigorous administrative occupation of Korea stemmed in part from Japan's intention to exploit the colony maximally within the briefest period of time to meet domestic economic needs. It was also the result of a colonial ruling style that rarely sought cooperation with groups in the colonized society.

This situation was otherwise rare in modern colonial history. Since the time of Cortés' alliance with the Aztec vassal subgroup of the Totonacs in 1519, colonial conquerors repeatedly exploited antagonisms among their opponents and mobilized relief troops and porters on the spot. After the period of conquest, "collaboration" proved essential. Colonial systems were virtually never able to be supported solely by enforcements from the mother country. When small foreign groups of functionaries ruled over large overseas populations for an extended period of time, dominion was based on a specific mix of five factors:[95] 1) the threat and employment of force by colonial security forces; 2) the adoption of traditional roles and symbols by the highest representatives of the colonial state; 3) "communication imperialism": the systematic collection, processing, and dissemination of information about the colonized society by centralized institutions; 4) a calculated strategy of "divide and conquer"; and 5) an aspiration for the continued existence of the colonial system on the part of influential segments of the colonial society. This interest was nurtured by the colonial power, and constituted a prerequisite for "collaboration."

Collaboration is thus only one of at least five factors, the most heavily analyzed and yet the least clarified of these factors. The term "collaboration" has become established for what might better be described as a *convergence of interests* between colonial state and individual groups or classes of colonized society. "Collaboration" is an unfortunate choice of term. It inevitably recalls the treacherous cooperation of individuals and small cliques with a military occupation regime hated by the remainder of the subjugated population during World War II, causing untold damage to their compatriots. In the colonial context few examples come to mind for which this kind of analogy would be appropriate, other than the isolated instance of an informant or a native member of the security forces who voluntarily served the colonial power in a period of extreme anti-colonial polarization. Unambiguous friend-or-foe situations and deliberate treachery accompanied the rise of anti-colonial nationalism in the early twentieth century. Until then, rule by foreigners was not necessarily considered *illegitimate* foreign rule. We cannot assume that in 1913 in Togo the Germans were *detested* as they were in 1943 in the Netherlands, nor can we assert that the majority of the Indians viewed British rule as alien tyranny.

How can an expanded concept of "indigenous collaboration," dissociated from the connotation of treason, be applied to a colonial context? The first step is to differentiate collaboration in a patron-client relationship from collaboration in a system of domination.

Clientelism exists when the weaker partner is dependent on the stronger without being at the stronger partner's mercy and directly subject to proconsular rule. The Roman empire surrounded itself with semi-autonomous clientele states and tribes that it did not need to rule since it could manipulate them.[96] This manipulation was possible because the clientele rulers knew how to couple their own benefit with that of the empire and get both accepted by the indigenous society. In this sense, King Herod I of Judea was arguably the best known collaborator of all time. "Informal empire" was also based on this type of collaboration, which empires welcomed as an inexpensive and unencumbered means of securing their interests. Major examples of collaboration elites or regimes within a patron-client relationship were the Chinese Qing Dynasty between about 1860 and 1900, the Khedives of Egypt before 1879, and the oligarchies in the independent Latin American states of the nineteenth century that were oriented to the world market. By extending the concept, we may include Siam after 1851 and Japan after 1868, where elites in both countries, in reaction to international pressure, modernized their lands in partial cooperation with the western powers. Early modern trade with Asia and the delivery of slaves by African rulers to European slave traders were also based on convergences of interests that we may designate as "collaboration," even if the concept is thereby strained to its limit.

Collaboration in a colony, with its *system of domination*, is determined by dependencies of another sort. It originates in an encounter of disparate intentions. The colonial state seeks ways of attaining its goals at minimal cost by using available mechanisms of indigenous politics, while all groups and classes of the subjugated society face the necessity of developing survival strategies when encountering a new regime based on overwhelming power. This dilemma applies above all to the pre-colonial elites, who see their political legitimacy, their social status, and even their physical existence fundamentally threatened.

In the phase of conquest, the colonial power seeks military *allies*. They are often dropped as soon as they have done their part. In the subsequent consolidation phase, the colonial state often, though not always, strives for alliances with indigenous groups. These groups have nothing in common but their function: to aid the colonial state in acquiring information and resources (especially taxes and labor services). Even though a cooperation of this sort cannot be interpreted as an ethical betrayal of an entirely voluntary nature, it does not come to pass by sheer coercion. Colonial collaboration entails a degree of *reciprocity*. The collaborators anticipate an elevation of their personal status, financial gain, or the security that the colonial state will provide protection against their rivals. Seen from one perspective, this collaboration seems like ingratiation to the colonial state, but it can also be viewed as a traditional quest for patronage.

Collaborators are also, at least in our definition, *semi-autonomous agents*, not appointed functionaries or cogs in the colonial mechanism. Instead, they stand at the relay point between colonial state and colonized society. They are middlemen who have one foot in each of the two camps. It would be excessive to characterize Indian Sepoy soldiers on the British payroll or Senegalese telegraphists as "collaborators." To at least some extent, collaboration must be actual, not just ornamental. Native puppet rulers who were retained in office pro forma had only a symbolic function.

The intentions of the invaders and the type of indigenous society determine the manner in which a given collaborative relationship is achieved. Three basic types of collaborative situations may be distinguished: 1) In hierarchically ordered societies, colonial powers often replaced only the top posts of the *ancien régime* and then stabilized parts of the old landed upper class by granting privileges in exchange for anticipated tax income. This was the course of events with the Zamindars in Bengal.[97] 2) A more drastic outcome was likely if the old ruling class had violently opposed the conquest or for other reasons appeared inappropriate as a collaboration elite. It was then altogether stripped of power, as evidenced in Algeria, Burma, and Vietnam (especially in its southern part, Cochin China). A collaborative association had to be built up "from below" during a phase of direct foreign rule with new societal forces. Frequently, newly converted Catholics assumed this role in Vietnam.[98] 3) When conquerors were unable to discern the structures of authority in the societies they had acquired, they were unsure of how to impose a hierarchical colonial system of rule. The British encountered this difficulty in the Punjab, where there was no obvious local master class analogous to the Bengali Zamindars. "Tribe" and "clan" leaders were sought in vain until finally a kind of landed gentry was actually "invented" by legal regulations.[99] Africa had numerous other examples of the creation of "kings," "chiefs," and other responsible partners by colonial powers.

This process of concretizing novel structures of authority, even if they were often misinterpreted as "typically African" by the colonizers, was a component of the revolution that signalled colonialism, particularly in Africa. Disarmament of the natives and successful assertion of the colonial state's monopoly on power shifted political coordinates so as to invalidate all pre-colonial standards. In the view of some segments of the African population, the white governor was the true heir of the earlier warrior chieftains. The old authorities lost their military might and ruling charisma. The chiefs, whether legitimated traditionally by succession or installed artificially, quickly became the tools of the colonial state, even if the state temporarily depended on their services for lack of a "petit personnel blanc" to mobilize a workforce, collect taxes, or organize transfers of land. Especially when European district officers returned the favor by closing their eyes to abuses of power by native counterparts, the latter risked their remaining legitimacy with the population—and with it their usefulness as mainstays of the colonial system. Herein lay the fundamental contradiction of every collaborative relationship. The ability of the native chief or the village elders to fulfill the demands of the colonial state was predicated on an independent position of respect, which was undermined by these very demands. A fully discredited collaborator was worthless. He had done his duty.

Territorial Bureaucratic State and Nation

A momentous effect of colonialism was its contribution to universalizing the European concept of the state. Only centralized autocracies, such as the Indian Mughal empire, were pre-colonial states in an even remotely modern sense. Political rule elsewhere in Asia and Africa was informal, personal, imbedded in cults and religion, unstable, malleable, and negotiable between power groups. It was more a network of loyalties than a configuration of solid institutions. The colonial state of the nineteenth and twentieth centuries, a secularized bureaucratic state supported by the military, was the opposite; it spawned forms of bureaucratic rule that contributed to the development of authoritarian systems in Asia and Africa.

When late colonial attempts at representative democracy after independence persevered, as in India, an underpinning of political ideas and political culture was frequently lacking. The colonial system lived on in the
framework of democratic institutions as "the model of the state which
exists for its own sake."[100]

The colonial state brought about the universal acceptance of the territorial principle. In Africa, above all, defining state borders was one of the
most consequential activities of the Europeans. The fact that these borders were drawn arbitrarily, as is often pointed out, did not impede their
widespread acknowledgement by the independent states. Often, the borders were not fully accepted until the post-colonial period. Just because a
colonial state was a *territorial* state, it was by no means automatically a
nation-state. The idea of a nation was more a weapon in the anti-colonial
struggle. The leaders of emancipation, who inherited the bureaucratic territorial state, interpreted it as a nation-state, or even as a state of the predominant ethnic group. Many of today's ethnic and religious conflicts can
be explained by this separate genealogy of the territorial and the national
principle and by their lack of congruence. Whereas the European colonial
powers—like all administrators of empires—had tolerated the diversity
of plural societies or even supported them in the spirit of the "divide and
conquer" principle, post-colonial politics often adopted the homogeniz-
ing claims to exclusivity of the European concept of "one state, one
nation." In this way nation-states developed that were not supported by
deeply rooted nations.

VI

Colonial Forms of Economy

African slaves work a Barbados refinery, where sugar cane is turned into sugar, molasses, and rum for the trans-Atlantic triangular trade.

(Dutertre, Histoire Generale des Antilles, 1667)

Even when a colony was not primarily acquired for economic reasons, extensive effects on the economy of the region in question were inevitable. The establishment of colonial rule was one of the most important means of acquiring natural resources and human labor to foster intercontinental trade, which accelerated during the early modern period. The economic effects of colonialism on the periphery varied vastly by time and place; West Africa differed greatly from East Africa, as did Sumatra from Java.

In America, conquest paved the way for affiliation with the international economic system. In the Old World, the reverse was true. In Asia and Africa, only sparsely populated or remote areas with few resources had not established foreign trade contacts before the colonial period. Long before their subjection to colonial rule, large parts of Africa had had intensive interaction with other continents, first in transatlantic and oriental slave trade and later with "legitimate" trading of goods (palm products, for instance). New opportunities to acquire wealth at the coast became an important source of domestic African societal dynamics. After 1890, the colonial rulers in West Africa and other overseas regions simply forged ahead with older trends in the development of the export economy.[101] There were also clear continuities extending well beyond the various decolonizations. As the example of post-colonial Latin America after 1825 proves, the end of a colonial system of domination in no way implies the end of world economic dependency. The countries of the later "Third World" that remained politically independent did not follow a fundamentally different path of development than that of the colonies. (Japan was an exception.) Colonialism is therefore only one among many facets of the more comprehensive history of economic relations between north and south.[102]

Imperial and colonial economic policies

In many cases, a phase of anarchic plundering followed on the heels of colonial conquest. It was a phase of unchecked economic and ecological devastation with ruinous exploitation of easily obtained resources. Only with the stabilization of colonial political structures were the prerequisites set for more systematic economic utilization, which French colonial theory labeled "mise en profit."

The establishment of a colonial economy necessitates gaining sovereignty over taxes as well as foreign trade and currency, which is perhaps the lowest common denominator of its manifold forms. In this way, self-financing of the colonial state and linking of the colony to external markets was made possible. Particularly in the exploitation colonies, the financial basis of the system stemmed in part from direct taxation of property and in part from a poll tax or exactment per housing unit. Later, indirect consumer taxes were added, the levying of which was often leased to private individuals in Asia, for example in the form of opium monopolies.[103] The importance of customs revenue grew with the volume of foreign trade. Colonial taxes were not necessarily higher than the tributes of the pre-colonial period. However, they were imposed with greater regularity and efficiency, without regard for the taxpayer's ability to pay. Taxpayers in the pre-colonial "moral economy" were often able to count on leniency in times of crisis. Colonial taxation led to the expansion of the money economy and market relations. It could be an effective instrument to mobilize workers without resorting to force. If workers wanted to earn cash to pay their taxes, they had to leave the closed circle of the subsistence economy.[104] Traditional community structures could be dismantled, since it was no longer a village or another collective that was assessed, but the individual household.

Without exception, foreign trade in the colonies was in the hands of foreign businessmen, acting as royal officials, chartered companies, specialized colonial agencies, or multinational concerns. Political control was reserved for the colonial, or, to be more precise, imperial state. The forms and intensity of this control evolved over time. After the early modern era of monopolies, from the mid-nineteenth century to the Great Depression of the 1930s, came an age of free trade (nearly unlimited in the British, Dutch, and Belgian colonies, but less consistent in the French colonies), and then a late phase of managed economy. Each of these trade regimes was geared to the advantage of the colonial power, not to the economic independence of the native population.

The sturdiest economic links within the empires were monetary ties. Through colonialism, Africa acquired currencies in the modern sense for the first time. France went to the greatest lengths to build a monetarily unified colonial empire, which gave it particular flexibility. This system proved to be so favorable for the colonies that after independence, the Francophone states of Africa maintained their close currency ties to France. Most of the former British colonies, on the other hand, opted for monetary autonomy. Because currency management in the British Empire was firmly interconnected once the Indian rupee was based on the pound sterling in 1893, monetary questions became a locus of controversy between the colonial power and nationalist critics of its politics. The entanglement of colonies in international money and currency relations became manifest during the Great Depression.

When colonial states saw the development of export potential as their primary economic aim, they pursued infrastructural projects as the most direct means of attaining it. Export sectors nearly always required extensive government investments. In India, Java, and parts of Africa, efficient railway systems were in operation by the outbreak of World War I. The construction of the Indian railroads was rightly called "the most monumental project of the colonial era."[105] Nearly as monumental were the reclamation of land by British construction of canals in the North and West of India and the French irrigation systems in Vietnam, which made the Mekong Delta one of the world's most productive regions for rice cultivation. By developing harbor facilities, the colonial state also created conditions for the private enterprise upsurge in colonial foreign trade. Steamship travel to the colonies and the development of telegraph networks—at the turn of the century, all large colonial centers could be reached by cable from London or Paris—were subsidized by the national governments.

Rural Agriculture[106]

The vast majority of people in colonized societies earned their livelihood from growing crops. Socially and culturally, they belonged to a rural milieu. Subsistence agriculture was not necessarily the only type of farming, however. In the cultural centers of Asia, production for local and distant markets was highly developed long before the advent of colonialism. Agriculture in some areas of Africa, which was more sparsely settled, had also begun to react to market stimuli. Colonial conquest had a twofold impact: it forcibly seized rural means of production, and it pursued agrarian commercialization.

In many areas overseas, the conquerors initially sought ways to have the indigenous population work for them. Rarely was there a complete enslavement of the natives over a prolonged period, but in nearly all cases there were forms of unfree labor. Characteristic for Spanish America in the sixteenth century was the assignment of Native American workers to private individuals by the crown (*encomienda*). Initially, this system rivalled slavery in the degree of coercion and brutality. In time, the *encomienda* rights came under increasing state control. Eventually, the Spanish required little compulsory labor from the Native Americans but instead taxed them in commodities and money tributes. Under the subsequent system of the *repartimiento* (called *mita* in Peru), every Native American community had to assign part of its male population to labor away from home in regular intervals. This practice became most oppressive in Peru when silver was mined in Potos'. While it continued there until the end of the colonial period, workers in Central Mexico were free from all but economic pressures by 1800.[107]

Slavery existed in all early modern empires until the abolitionist movement of the nineteenth century. In the Old World, however, slavery never had a major role in agricultural production. Nineteenth-century colonialism, which at times derived its own justification by virtue of its opposition to *oriental* forms of slavery (in East Africa, for instance), did not dispense with unfree labor. To be sure, the brutal excesses in the Congo Free State, which was a private colony of King Leopold II of Belgium, were atypical. However, everywhere in Africa there were forms of unpaid and paid *corvée* and compulsory porter services; the deployment of African soldiers at the scenes of both world wars also comes to mind in this context. The last large-scale attempt to implement forced labor in Asia before the Japanese practice of ruinous exploitation during World

War II was the Dutch "Culture System" of the years 1830-1870, in which Javanese coffee in particular was grown for export under a *repartimiento*-like regime of communal work mobilization.

Even more prevalent than forced labor was loss of access to the soil, which almost invariably caused irreversible pauperization. It was the norm in settlement colonies of the "New England" type, in which the suppressed natives were rarely farmers. There was large-scale expropriation of land in Algeria and South Africa, and to a lesser extent in Kenya, Rhodesia, and New Zealand, with the direct help of the colonial state, itself often little more than an instrument of the settlers. The highest quality land thus wound up in the hands of foreigners. West Africa by contrast remained peasant country, protected by a different kind of colonial politics. Paradoxically, the Mexican Indians lost large parts of their country *after* the burden of forced labor had been lifted. In the late colonial period, territorial expansion of large-scale *haciendas* at the expense of the property of village communities and small farmers commenced, and continued nearly unchecked until the early twentieth century. The small farmers were thereby marginalized as farm hands, half-share tenants, or itinerant workers.[108] The Mexican Indios lost control over their own manner of living not with early colonial forced labor, which left the Indian community basically intact, but with expropriation of land by semi-capitalist *haciendas*.[109]

Even if the colonial state in India or West Africa did not always require the manpower of the farmers or confiscate their land, it still entangled them in the delicate net of its supervision. Where habits, traditions, and loose arrangements had once sufficed, land registers, demarcations of open fields, tax assessments, property titles, and countless regulations now took over. Agrarian or peasant societies were themselves in a way by-products of colonialism.[110] In the course of extensive revamping of production for the world market, which began in Asia during the last third of the nineteenth century and in sub-Saharan Africa during the first decade of the twentieth century and involved the extension and intensification of agriculture, the economic principle of developed colonialism was realized: "a reallocation of resources within the agrarian sector from a variety of nonagrarian tasks (rural industry) to increased specialization of export products."[111] Many highly specialized cash crop regions were no longer able even to cover their requirements for foodstuffs from their own production. With an increasing division of labor, these societies became more "modern," but at the same time more closely geared toward agricultural production. Export production within the framework of the rural family had quite disparate effects on the agrarian systems specific to different countries. In general, a more distinct and stable social stratification developed with more pronounced differences between rich and poor. An individual's range of experience now transcended the local sphere. Village structures were more clearly defined, particularly since almost all colonial powers strengthened or even created the office of the village head. Restless nomadism was repressed. In many West African countries the small rural family business, which knew how to adapt to the market situation, profited from the export boom. By contrast, in a hierarchical order landlordism as in Cochin China, in the southern part of Vietnam, only a tiny class of parasitic absentee landowners benefitted. The mass of indebted tenant farmers had to continue eking out a meager existence.[112]

Capitalist Production

Two diametrically opposed forms of enterprise, the farm household and the plantation, were and still are the most efficient bases of the agrarian export economy. The farm household cultivates its own and/or rented land with family members and perhaps a small number of paid workers. The *plantation* is a large-scale enterprise, often remotely situated. Its construction requires substantial capital investments in land, machines, and plants and is kept in operation by often incompetent wage laborers under the direction of a foreign management. Plantations are often owned by foreign stock corporations, which also manages the processing and marketing of products. The plantation is "capitalist" without being *a priori* a more "rational" form of enterprise than the market-oriented farm household. In Africa, the modern tropical plantation had a pivotal role for only a brief period, mainly in Cameroon, whereas this type of plantation was extensively developed in Southeast Asia (producing caoutchouc [India rubber], sugar, tobacco, coffee, and copra) and in Ceylon (producing coffee and tea).

The Asiatic caoutchouc plantation, which owed its prosperity to the increased availability of the automobile, followed the organization of the Caribbean plantation, an advanced capitalist institution of early modern times. Philip Curtin attributes six features to the full-fledged Atlantic plantation of the seventeenth and eighteenth centuries: 1) slave labor; 2) demographic insufficiency, requiring constant recruitment of new workers; 3) large-scale organization with fifty to five hundred workers and a strict timetable for production; 4) "feudal" sovereign power of the plantation owner, sometimes over life and death; 5) supply of an overseas market; and 6) political control over the system from Europe.[113] All but the first of these characteristics also apply to the plantations that arose after the late nineteenth century. The labor conditions on the plantations of East Sumatra in 1920 did not differ fundamentally from those in Jamaica or Saint Domingue two centuries earlier. The workers were recruited not locally, but from the neighboring island of Java or from as far away as South China ("foreigners," mainly Indians, also worked on the plantations in Malaya). Workers, capital, and management all had to be imported. The working conditions, harsh and racist through and through, as well as the sheer pressure of exploitation, scarcely differed from legally sanctioned slavery.[114]

Farms differ from plantations in four respects. On farms, the crops are less work intensive, the business is run not by employed managers and agents, but by the permanently resident owner family, production is not exclusively for export, but partly for domestic markets, and farms are generally not established as enclaves in remote areas or, like the caoutchouc plantations of Sumatra, in frontier wildernesses, but where farmers compete with indigenous peasants for meager land resources in a "zero sum" relationship. Like plantations, farms also employ wage laborers, but in much smaller proportion to the total expenditure.

In Africa, farms gave rise to extensive annexation of land, comparable to the Latin American haciendas, which dominated dependent workers in an even tighter way. These annexations are explained in part by an extensive type of agriculture (cattle breeding, corn, tobacco) and partly by the attitudes of European colonists, whose ideal Africa would have been an Africa without Africans. The plantation is based on the combination of high capital investment and exploitation of the cheap labor of "coolies" or day laborers of foreign races. The typical colonial farm, by contrast, is run with the help of European immigrant workers, as was the case with North American indentured service. In Africa, high quality indigenous labor was generally available for low wages, leaving no room in the labor market for white farm workers. At least in East Africa, handicraft and retail trade were under the control of efficiently managed Asiatic (mostly Indian) immigrants. In Africa, therefore, at least south of the Sahara, the conditions for full-fledged colonist societies, for a "new Australia," as it were, were lacking.[115] Economically, the settler farms perched precariously between native and international competition. On the *local* level, they had to deal with native competition, which developed into a kind of rural bourgeoisie in places like Kenya. When they tried to supply *international* markets, they competed with large-scale producers from other continents. The settlers could only offset their economic weakness by their privileged access to the colonial state.[116] The African farm never became an engine of growth in the manner of capitalist agrarian enterprises in North America and tropical plantations.

As of the late nineteenth century, Africa's significance for the world economy was not in agriculture, but in mining (gold, diamonds, copper, etc.),[117] roughly like the role of Peru and later Mexico in silver mining. In Asia, aside from the production of petroleum, mining for export has seldom attained a prominent position. Malayan tin and coal production in Manchuria, which was colonized by the Japanese, was the exception. Advanced capitalist African mining brought about extraordinary sociohistorical changes in its immediate vicinity.[118] The Belgian Congo (Zaire), which was rich in raw materials, temporarily achieved high economic growth rates. However, the enclaves of growth, which stood predominantly under the control of large foreign corporations, remained isolated from their rural surroundings. Largely as a result of post-colonial mismanagement, Zaire is today one of the world's poorest countries. Traces of industrialization were found in French West Africa after World War I. Only in South Africa did the transition to industrialization succeed. It was initiated by gold mining in the 1920s, after de facto independence had been attained in 1910. The price of this success was the immense social cost of an ever tenser racial dictatorship.

It is equally true of Asia that while the European colonial powers did not explicitly prevent industrialization, they failed to support it to any significant extent.[119] Only India had an expandable industrial sector at the time of its independence; this sector also included heavy industry. It was indebted to both Indian and British private enterprise initiatives.[120] The Japanese empire was a curious exception. Japan was the only imperial power that systematically built up an *industrial* colonial economy in its colonial empire as well as in the zones of informal penetration: coal, iron, and steel in Korea and Manchuria, sugar in Taiwan, and cotton processing in Shanghai and North China. The plan was to supplement the economy of the Japanese islands, which were poor in natural resources, and help the planned Asian "coprosperity sphere," dominated by Japan, establish an autarky based on a division of labor. Although Japanese colonialism may have been the most repressive colonial regime in recent history and the suppressed people had not the least reason to be grateful to their oppressors, their material and structural legacy was an important basis for further industrial development in Korea, Taiwan, and parts of China.[121]

Its many agrarian and industrial variants notwithstanding, colonial capitalism (with the possible exception of Indian industry) had two basic features. For one, it was created not by capital accumulation on the spot, but by foreign investments, resulting in some degree of foreign control. A racial antagonism was superimposed on the social conflict between entrepreneurs and a working class that hardly ever unionized. For another, the forms of work that colonial capitalism entailed were never quite comparable to "free wage labor" in the modern western sense. Foreign entrepreneurs used the non-economic pressures common to pre-colonial societies for their own purposes. Wages continued to be paid partly in commodities. Despite the rudiments of a reign of law, management, with or without the help of the colonial state, had more severe means of disciplining workers than could be applied in metropolitan capitalism.

Colonial Societies

Anglo-Indian dinner in the mid-nineteenth century

(Curry and Rice Illustration, India)

America was not only a newly *discovered* world for Europeans; it was also a world whose society they *restructured*. The *North* American colonies began as offshoots of Europe, and although they remained neo-European in ethnic respects, sociocultural forms developed that left these origins far behind.[122] Alexis de Tocqueville made this clear in his incomparable *De la démocratie en Amérique* (1835-1840).

In the three culture areas of the American *South* that were shaped by Europe—Brazil, the Caribbean, and the Hispano-American mainland down to Paraguay—societies of an altogether different type evolved, departing still further from European models. These ethnically and culturally heterogeneous societies comprised Native American, European, and African elements.[123] The ethnically inclusive South stood in contrast to the ethnically exclusive North. Although the main social cleavage in the South divided the white master class from the rest of the population, in practice stratification by skin color developed within roughly the first century after the conquista, especially in the colonial Spanish area. The finely graded hierarchy ranged from the "pureblooded" Spanish to the Native American masses.[124] This "pigmentocracy" was complicated by two factors. For one, "race" and "class" correlated in most, but not all cases. The number of poor whites grew while a middle class of mestizos and emancipated black slaves arose, which comprised several additional subcategories.[125] For another, *cultural* proximity to the Spanish language, dress, and behavior often mattered more than the physical degree of skin pigmentation. In the late eighteenth century, a legal means of having oneself declared "white" was even opened to rich and educated mulattos. Whether a new type of "mestizo society," distinct from a colonial society, actually originated in Mexico and nowhere else in Latin America is open to speculation.[126] The only enduring certainty over the course of centuries was the material and cultural deprivation of the Indios.

In the Caribbean and Brazilian centers of plantation slavery, in which an absolute bipartite division of the population into a white master class and black slave masses might be expected, circumstances were anything but clear. Since all of the slavery regimes provided for setting some slaves free right from the start, there was a third group: the "freed colored class."[127] This process of emancipation was less evident in the highly racist French, British, and Dutch colonies than in the Iberian territories. After the murder or flight of the white planters, the great slave uprising in St. Domingue of 1791 was directed especially at the small class of affluent mulatto plantation owners who had themselves been the targets of judicial discrimination in the past. In the whole Caribbean, stratification by color has continued even after the era of slavery and the colonial period had come to an end.

Ethnocultural Demarcation in the Old World

Caribbean slave societies were "an artificial and novel construct in the history of European imperialism."[128] By contrast, societies in the Old World did not emerge as the result of European expansion, with the possible exception of South Africa. In the Old World, colonialism did not *create* societies; it only *reshaped* existing "traditional" societies, sometimes partially and superficially as in Cambodia, sometimes radically as in neighboring Cochin China. Within the territorial borders of Asian and African colonies, there were no multicultural societies of Europeans and native inhabitants that would have been viable after independence. Whether the intruders were small groups of bureaucrats and soldiers in the exploitation colonies or larger colonist communities in the settlement colonies of the "African" type, they stayed aloof from the native population. There was, of course, sexual contact. The sexual exploitation of native women was nothing out of the ordinary for them. Sensual temptations abroad may even have propelled the colonial desire for adventure,[129] but interracial liaisons of any sort were increasingly considered illegitimate. Besides a heightened moral awareness fostered by vigilant missionaries, the colonists assumed that a lack of sexual distance would detract from the "racial prestige" of the white rulers and thereby weaken their aura as an incorruptible master class.[130] The racially mixed part of the population never attained sufficient demographic weight to become politically significant. Status and living conditions of mestizo "Eurasians" in the Asiatic colonial world deteriorated in the transition to the nineteenth century and grew markedly worse than those of Euro-Africans in the Caribbean possessions after the epoch of slavery.

Asian and African colonies failed to develop integrated colonial societies with relatively homogeneous elites and widely accepted cultures. The basic model of colonial sociology was instead as follows: Within the system of domination set up and maintained by the colonial state, two distinct social structures came into contact without modifying one another, namely the majority indigenous society (which was initially "traditional") and the minority society of the colonial rulers and settlers. This latter society was a mere sociocultural bridgehead of the metropolis and had no "Creole" identity. Between these two evolved the overlapping area of the actual colonial society, in which new intermediary social roles emerged: missionaries, interpreters, commercial middlemen, political "collaborators," and so on.

This area of intersection between metropolitan and indigenous societies was also marked by social and ethnic distance, which explains why scarcely any social disentanglement was required when the exploitation colonies were later decolonized. The European, American, and Japanese colonial rulers packed their bags and vanished, leaving only a collection of architectonic shells—public buildings, villas, monumental cemeteries, memorials, entire townscapes—as well as landscapes from which the careful observer can detect the effects of ecological devastation as well as the successes of early efforts at conservation.[131] Settlers defended their position, which was based on immobile property, more persistently than administrators. For this reason and others, the emancipation of settlement colonies often proceeded more violently than that of exploitation colonies. In cases like Algeria, the colonist society and the indigenous society were more closely enmeshed. Their separation was literally a more painful process.

Social proximity within the colonial relationship varied from one historical period to another. One factor that indicated social affinities and distances was the degree of "counter-acculturation" of colonizers to colonized. The Trek Boers were partially "Africanized," the Spaniards living in remote rural areas of America who had already lost Spanish as a mother tongue in the second generation became "Indianized," European vocabulary was flavored with native words,[132] Creole and pidgin languages developed, and "barbarian" habits such as betel nut chewing were taken up by the refined Dutch and half-Dutch ladies of Batavia. This counter-acculturation rarely altered the core of cultural identity, however; hardly ever did Europeans convert to non-Christian religions of their own accord.

Characteristic of the social and cultural history of modern colonialism, especially in Asia, was the increasing alienation between two societies that had shared the bond of a colonial relationship since the late eighteenth century. While the status scale in Iberian America was rapidly refined, thereby placing renewed emphasis on racial criteria, the dualization of the colonial social landscape intensified in Asia and Africa. Only in Portuguese Asia was there significant progress in societal interaction, especially where native clergy were concerned, owing to the enlightened politics of the crown under the Marquis de Pombal in the 1760s and 1770s.[133] The sealing off of the European communities from the indigenous environment had many causes, which were manifested in varying combinations: 1) Although Portugal and the Netherlands in particular had officially encouraged marriage between European men and Asian women at first, and the other colonial powers had tolerated it tacitly, immigration of European women raised the sexual autarky of the colonial societies. 2) The transition from trade to rule and often to direct production with dependent workers transformed the "age of partnership"[134] into an age of subordination. 3) Violent resistance by the natives, such as the Native American massacre of colonists in Virginia in 1622 and the Indian rebellion of 1857-1858, strengthened the resolve of white minorities to shield themselves for self-protection. 4) A European attitude of superiority over the rest of the world, stemming from the Christian Eurocentricism of early encounters, made it appear increasingly "unreasonable" to Europeans to maintain close egalitarian relationships with non-Europeans and to make cultural accommodations to them. 5) After the gradual abolition of slave trade and slavery, racist thought lived on in less blatant, but now "scientifically" legitimated forms. It bears pointing out, however, that racism is often not the *cause* of segregation, but the *effect*. Racism has often been used to justify segregation after the fact.[135]

Ethnosocial distancing was an outgrowth of societal interaction and was not always based on discriminatory laws. A telling example was Batavia, the most populous and resplendent city in Asia that was governed by Europe. In the first half of the seventeenth century, a mixed society was formed based on house slavery and the expansion of "Creole" family and patronage networks with relatively high tolerance for interracial family relationships. This society resembled its counterpart in Mexico and was even more akin to Portuguese colonization in Asia (Goa). In the manner of living of its upper class, the mixed society of Batavia conformed almost as closely to its Javanese surroundings as it did to Holland. A distinct demarcation between the European and Asian spheres commenced with the British interregnum of 1811-1816. In the eyes of the British, the Batavian Dutch were appallingly infected by their contact with Asians. Cultural decontamination was decreed. The whites in the city and their mestizo relatives were told to develop an identity as civilized Europeans and clearly display it in their appearances before the Javanese public.[136]

The English in India had always been somewhat more detached from the indigenous environment than the Dutch in Indonesia. After the 1780s, their isolation gradually intensified and became obvious with the decline in status of Eurasian Anglo-Indians, even though some influential Indian politicians in 1830 were still dreaming of a racially mixed India modelled on Mexico.[137] The club became the center of British social life in India and the other Asian colonies during the Victorian era. In clubs, one could feel like a gentleman among other gentlemen while being served by a native staff. In Kuala Lumpur, very few non-Europeans were admitted before 1940; in Singapore no non-Europeans were allowed in at all. The large clubs of Calcutta remained closed to Indians until 1946.[138] This type of color bar was especially disturbing because it excluded from social recognition the very people who had carried their self-Anglicizing the furthest and loyally supported British rule. Even Indian members of the Indian Civil Service were excluded.[139]

In most regions of Africa, the colonial period began at a time when exclusionist thought and action were most pronounced. In Africa there was virtually no history of intercultural proximity and therefore no need for policies enforcing detachment. The Europeans saw themselves as foreign rulers separated from the African cultures by an abyss. This absolute aloofness extended even to Islam, which they certainly did not consider "primitive," but rather historically obsolete. Color bars in Africa varied in height; they were lowest in West Africa and highest in the settlement colonies of the far north and the deep south. A process of great symptomatic significance was the rejection of the highly educated West Africans who had worked with the early mission. They had envisioned the colonial takeover as an opportunity for a joint European-African effort to modernize and civilize Africa.[140] Instead, they were now, as "white Negroes," despised by all.

Colonial Cities and Plural Societies

The colonial city is the ideal locus to study ethnic and social distance as the sociological core of colonialism in the nineteenth and twentieth centuries.[141] Colonial cities had their unvarying landmarks: churches, government buildings and consulates, customs houses, train stations, barracks, and racetracks as well as the occasional golf course in the British Empire. Their basic organizing principle was a segregation of residential quarters along racial lines. This segregation was partly the result of deliberate policies and partly of unplanned developments. In eighteenth-century Calcutta, which had been founded by the British in 1690, a "white town" and a "black town" sprang up adjacently. In the old Mughal city of Delhi, the British settled within the city walls, but after the 1870s they laid out separate residential districts. In Kingston, Jamaica, white flight from integrated neighborhoods was completed by about the same time. Beginning in the 1880s, urban separation was propagated in French Africa as well. This type of separation could be achieved most easily in cities that were systematically designed right from the start, notably Dakar, Nairobi, Singapore, and the splendid new residences of Rabat and New Delhi. The European districts were spacious, laid out as villas and bungalows on ample lots. Wherever possible, they were elevated and equipped with elaborate sewage systems. European sectors therefore enjoyed more sanitary conditions than the cramped indigenous districts, which were usually constructed at lower elevations near water. Occasionally private social reform initiatives by doctors and engineers led to considerable improvements of the sanitary conditions in the native areas as well, as was the case in Bombay. Economic geography was often marked by the contrast between bazaar and office.

It would be a gross oversimplification to designate all colonial cities as "dual cities."[142] A broad and subtly differentiated spectrum of rights and privileges was created by sensitive urban planning, as in Delhi when it became the capital of India in 1912.[143] In general, the colonial city should be characterized as plural, as an environment for more than two ethnic groups.[144] Legendary metropolises like Shanghai and Casablanca were not the first cosmopolitan melting pots and hubbubs. In Batavia (Jakarta), there were thousands of Chinese as well as hundreds of resident Arabs in addition to Dutch and Indonesians or Malays (who were further differentiated by origin). In the city of Singapore, which was designed from scratch, ethnic ghetto concentrations were introduced in 1823 that have left their mark on the cityscape even today. For Chinese, Indians, Bugis, Arabs (with mosque), and Europeans, the urban expanse provided zones for each group. Characteristically, as the Europeans grew more prosperous after about 1840, they moved away from the overcrowded waterfront and erected their villas in the middle of parks further inland.[145]

The "plural," multi-ethnic character of many colonies was most evident in their urban centers, but for two reasons was not limited to these. One reason was the combination of smaller socioethnic groups in a state with clearly defined boundaries; the other was migration movements, which may not have been triggered by colonialism, but were always intensified by them. Looking back on the modern history of colonization and colony building, its effect in mobilizing people may well be its most profound legacy, not only in America and Oceania, but also in Asia and Africa. The expansion of the Chinese into all regions of Southeast Asia began under the Tang Dynasty (seventh to tenth century), but only became a demographically significant mass phenomenon with the new economic opportunities afforded by the colonial economy in the nineteenth century. Indians settled by the hundred thousands in Burma, Malaya, East and South Africa, and on some of the Caribbean islands. Within Africa, permanent exodus and the creation of ethnic diasporas were rarer; when itinerant workmen, mostly young men, left their villages, they hoped to return. However, here too, the mobility level rose quite substantially in the early twentieth century, and polarizations ensued between poor countries of origin, such as Mozambique and Njasaland/Malawi, and the areas to which they were attracted by the availability of employment, such as jobs in mining and export-oriented agriculture.

In many colonies, immigrant minorities became commercial intermediaries. The ethnic diversity of the merchant groups in harbor cities such as Calicut and Malacca had been obvious to the European "discoverers" of Asia. Under modern colonialism, new opportunities for entrepreneurs arose in ethnic niches. The tin industry of Malaya was built up by Chinese and the batik textile production on Java taken over by Chinese; the religious rather than ethnic minority of the Parsees was involved from the beginning of the Indian cotton textile industry.

Not only was there an exodus of Europeans from indigenous neighborhoods; colonial governments also set great store by the separation of the non-white population groups from one another. This separation resulted in part from a well-calculated ruling technique, partly from the projection of new western criteria of ethnicity onto societies, the study of which now became the task of ethnologists and anthropologists. Whatever scholarship had distinguished on the basis of linguistic and social science criteria was now to be divided in practice as well. British indirect rule in the theoretical form it acquired at the turn of the century by Sir Frederick Lugard and the segregationist "politique des races" of some of his French contemporaries had this type of ethnological underpinning.[146]

An ambitious theory, developed by the British colonial official John S. Furnivall using the particular example of Burma, was the doctrine of the "plural society." This doctrine was later refined by M. G. Smith. By "plural society" Furnivall meant "a society . . . comprising two or more elements or social orders which live side by side, yet without mingling, in one political unit."[147] According to Furnivall, each element in the plural society pursued its own values and goals. A plural society lacked unifying bonds, such as religious ties and a common social will. The plural society was held together only by the power of the colonial state and by common economic interests, the market being the only meeting point for all of its constituents. This societal form was unstable by nature. M. G. Smith, who took the British Caribbean as his empirical illustration, strengthened the cultural dimension of the theory while downplaying its economic dimension, and noted a overriding tendency for one group to dominate the others in the cultural sphere.[148]

Furnivall's theory did not dispute the coercive character of the colonial state, but he viewed the Europeans as *one* ethnocultural element among others in colonial society. He thereby transcended the simplistic dichotomies of colonizers versus colonized and imperialists versus nationalists. Furnivall emphasized an important motif central to later radical critiques of colonialism: in his view, no segment of the plural colonial society was authentic and well-rounded in and of itself; individuals led "incomplete" social existences. The European, for example, "works in the tropics, but does not live there."[149] Furnivall's (and Smith's) remarkable theory has not gone uncriticized. It has been justly accused of ignoring politics, underestimating the role of elites, and undervaluing opportunities for consensus and potential for conflict.[150] However, many of the contradictory dynamics of plural societies as they are manifested in numerous ethnic and religious conflicts of the present often became virulent only during the actual decolonization process, after the period of colonial rule and even after a post-emancipatory transitional phase. For the sociology of colonialism itself, Furnivall's insights are still compelling.

VIII

Colonialism and
Indigenous Culture

A missionary school in the Belgian Congo

The West Indian author V. S. Naipaul has written: "The colonial, of whatever society, is a product of revolution; and the revolution takes place in the mind."[151] Revolution was initiated by contact with expansive western civilization. This contact seldom led to a complete collapse of pre-colonial cosmologies and ways of life, but always to its "destructuring" into fragments[152] or at least to a challenging of cultural values previously taken for granted. Individual and collective revolutionizing of consciousness followed from the perception of this challenge and an attempt to adjust to it. Usually, the reactions were in some way *creative*. Western civilization has hardly ever prevailed without being reshaped to some degree.

The colonial period was an important stage in the global process of westernization, although in many places the process began even *before* colonization (Egypt is an obvious case) and continued *after* independence from colonial rule. Westernization also took place in societies like Japan, which never fell to foreign rule. Indeed, there is much to support the view that the worldwide expansion of mass media and western consumer supplies in the past decades has transformed non-European civilizations more than centuries of colonial cultural modification.

This cultural modification was initiated by the colonial state, which intervened in indigenous cultures with varying degrees of intensity, depending on the intent and strategy of colonizing. Extreme examples could be found in close proximity.[153] In the Philippines—and of course also in America—the Spanish pursued an energetic politics of westernization as far back as the sixteenth century, whereas in Indonesia in the seventeenth and eighteenth centuries the Dutch went about their business without mingling in their cultural environment. Spanish became a colonial colloquial language, but Dutch did not until well into the nineteenth century.

The decisive variable was the role of the Christian *mission*. In the Iberian territories, the Catholic church was an integral part of the expansion project from the start. In the New World, it served the state as a powerful instrument of cultural penetration. In the Philippines, the power of the monastic orders surpassed the power of the secular state functionaries. The fragmented Philippine archipelago was the only area in Asia to become the target of a comprehensive Christian invasion.[154] The Catholic mission had been launched in the sixteenth century in a blaze of optimism. However, by the mid-nineteenth century, relatively little actual progress had been made. In America, the Catholic mission lost its impetus and frequently degenerated into an oppressive tyranny of priests. In Japan it failed because of political opposition; in China and Africa its successes remained minimal.

Throughout the colonial realm of the early Protestant powers, Christianizing and "civilizing" the natives were dispensed with. Attention was focused instead on maintaining the faith of the colonists, especially in the Dutch empire. The English East India Company observed a maxim of strict non-intervention in religious questions in the regions it ruled until 1813. The Puritans of New England considered the Native American inhabitants the "children of Satan" and therefore unworthy of proselytism. The later Protestant mission originated in the evangelical revival of the late eighteenth and nineteenth centuries, which was closely allied to the anti-slavery movement.[155]

The mission of the nineteenth and twentieth centuries cannot be sweepingly condemned as the tool of colonialism,[156] except perhaps in the case of France until (and frequently in spite of) the laicizing of the Third Republic. Sometimes the missionaries were brought in on warships; in other instances, their calls for help offered welcome reasons to intervene. It also happened (in the South Sea, for instance) that cunning native rulers roped in the missionaries for their own purposes as allies in an internal political power struggle. In general, missionaries of all faiths and nationalities supported colonial annexation, affirmed the colonial system on principle, and shared the cultural arrogance of their secular compatriots, which could escalate to brutal aggression toward non-European ways of life. However, time and again there were representatives of a missionary "left" who rejected the excesses of arbitrary colonial rule.

Earlier than others, they recognized the unstoppable trend toward emancipation after World War I and tried to indigenize the clergy.

The Protestant movement was organized in a large number of societies that differed in their goals and methods. Some of these organizations originated in non-colonial countries, and some, such as the American missionaries in China, were also active outside the regular colonial constellations.

The mission is an especially clear example of how unintended side effects and repercussions developed their own dynamics. Wolfgang Reinhard called this the "dialectics of colonialism."[157] The mission's effectiveness was confirmed not only or even primarily by its success in conversion, but also in the areas of education and social work. Secular western cultural values were transmitted as by-products of the primary intention to Christianize. In view of this overlap between secular and religious impulses, it is advisable not to differentiate so much by actors— colonial state or mission—as by fields of intercultural contact and conflict. The most important of these were religion and education.

Religion

Colonial regimes and missionaries acted to undermine native cults and religious convictions with differing degrees of zeal. The natives, in turn, proved resistent to quite varied degrees. From the meeting of these vectors, roughly four results were possible. Never did imported "modernity" and local "tradition" merely clash or co-exist. Instead, new blends evolved.

1) *Suppression of native cults and establishment of a state-supported Christian monopoly on religion.* The classic case was Mexico. The organizational backbone of Aztec "idol worship" was broken here by destroying temples and persecuting the priest caste. The country was overwhelmed with a tight church organization. Especially in the interior, the Indios fell under the "most dreadful despotism" of the monks.[158] The cultural baggage of early modern Europe was transported along with the monotheistic Christian religion, especially an individualist concept of human beings, the ideal of the nuclear family, a "civilized" view of the body and of sexuality, a linear notion of time, the need to record for pos-

terity, etc. However, fragments of the Indian religion lived on in practices, images, and symbols that infiltrated Christianity and led to syncretic blends. The Indios also reacted to non-religious elements of European perspectives with very creative results in assimilation and interpretation.[159] Similarily, in the Philippines, local and imported cultures blended and reblended.

2) *Self-Christianization and transition to indigenous churches.* The Protestant influence in Africa was essentially a process of self-Christianization and transition to indigenous churches. As in the case of America, syncretism was of pivotal importance, but it took a different form in Africa. The initial European missionary efforts of the years after 1860, which were less rigidly imposed by the state than in the Spanish colonies, were taken up in a second phase by the Africans themselves. The missionaries built the church organizations, and native assistants took over most of the preaching and converting. In a third phase, African churches were built. The Christian message thus raced ahead of its European preachers. It became an important inspiration for decolonization.

3) *Stimulation of non-Christian countermovements.* In a broad spectrum of cases, confrontations between differing views of life led not to Christianizing adapted to local conditions, but conversely to an (often unconscious) infusion of western Christian elements into religious attitudes that remained essentially non-Christian. In a crisis of cultural orientation, native religions were reformulated—often in order to brace their powers of resistance. When this reformulation involved a regression to magic, as in the East African Maji-Maji rebellion of 1905-1907 and in the anti-missionary Chinese Boxer Rebellion of the years 1898-1900, it could have disastrous consequences. European bullets could simply not be magically "liquified." Socioreligious reform movements promised greater success. They attempted a revival, renewal, or reinterpretation of older traditions by building on their own tradition of religious reform. Ironically, this quest for "authenticity" sometimes reflected an obsession of *western* orientalism (for instance, the academic discipline "history of religion") with genuine cultural "substances" that did not really exist in the religious medley of Asia. Thus, the notion of "Hinduism" as a clearly identifiable "world religion" whose doctrines can be neatly summarized was alien to pre-colonial India. "Hinduism" is nothing "but an orchid cul-

tivated by European science."[160] Since trends within Indian neo-Hinduism stood on precisely this type of foundation, they achieved a more decisive break with the past than their own programs had foreseen. Many varieties of anti-colonial solidarity were based on arbitrarily or non-arbitrarily "invented" religious and cultural traditions.[161] However, the conflict with the West not only spurred a new emphasis on autochthonous and particular traditions, sometimes in a radical fundamentalist shape, but also, in all Asiatic civilizations, inspired universalist currents of thought that sought a synthesis of the religious and philosophical traditions of East and West. Finally there were cases of frankly fabricated traditionless syncretism, such as the Vietnamese sect of Cao Dai, founded in 1926, which mingled Confucianism, Buddhism, Taoism, spiritism, and Freemasonry, among others, and added a quasi-Catholic church organization to the mixture. In politics it behaved opportunistically.

4) *Assertion or strengthening of the existing order.* Islam differed from all other religions with which missionaries and colonists came into contact. First, it proselytized and expanded on its own; second, it possessed a far more intensive history of contact with Christianity; and third, it remained essentially immune to efforts at Christianization. The attitude of the colonial powers was contradictory: On the one hand, they held to the old Crusades tradition of Christian anti-Islamism, on the other, they recognized that Muslim elites, particularly in Central Africa, India, and Malaya, were especially valuable partners in indirect rule. They had their hierarchically ordered local societies under predictable control. Where the colonial state did not advance with brute force against religion, law, and the educational system of the Muslims, as in Algeria, the Islamic way of life preserved its integrity to a high degree. In Malaya, for example, a majority of the population reacted to cultural pressure and (for some) the temptations of a western lifestyle by strengthening their identities as members of the Islamic community in a manner that was hardly noticeable on the outside. They also expanded sub-bureaucratic Islamic institutions. The result of colonialism was not the loss, but the strengthening of native culture.[162] Islam evolved in the process, of course. No other religion since the nineteenth century has worked at its relationship to the west so obsessively and with such divergent results in the spectrum between liberalism and fundamentalism. Although many Muslims con-

sidered themselves victims of European, then of American and Zionist colonialism, the fact remains that they displayed unusual resistance to the cultural values imported by the colonial powers.

Education[163]

Schools were the foremost mediators of these cultural values. They were run partly by missionaries and partly by the state. Some educational institutions were non-missionary private schools. France preferred a public instructional system, while Great Britain, Belgium, and Germany let the missions run the schools, providing only subsidies. Since education was usually not a priority for colonial politics, local variants were of all different types. Colonial "school" could range from a village gathering with an interpreter teaching the alphabet to urban model high schools with state-of-the-art pedagogy. Usually the most highly developed schools were in the secondary school system, as is also true of the early modern European history of education. The major beneficiaries of its facilities were the sons of the native urban middle classes. They were trained to be cadres in the lower ranks of the administration and to be employees of European firms. The ability to pay tuition fees determined an individual's chances for admission. The widespread regulation that required a metropolitan educational diploma for access to the higher colonial service had the practical effect of a racial barrier. Enrollment in schools or universities in France or England was, however, only available to a tiny upper-class segment of the population. Jawaharlal Nehru, the first president of independent India, educated at an exclusive English private school and at Cambridge University, was the son of a rich lawyer.

A broad elementary school education hardly existed in rural areas in the colonial world; the British in particular attached little importance to it until the late colonial period. Even when colonial rulers had the best of intentions, financial constraints prevented the realization of mass education programs. In French West Africa, a region with better than average educational institutions, matriculation in the 1930s was under four percent. Universities were founded only in the Spanish, English, and French empires. In the 1920s, Indonesia opened specialized post-secondary schools for technology, law, and medicine. The lucky few who had the opportunity to attend universities in Paris, Oxford, Leiden, or Lisbon were generally well received in Europe, but after returning to their colonial homeland, they found themselves downgraded once again to their former inferior status as "natives."

A notorious bone of contention was the language of instruction. Should the "cultured" language of the colonizers be used, or one of the colloquial languages? Teaching French to Africans would facilitate communication with them and was almost unavoidable if they were destined for public service, but it would also open up, so it was feared, access to subversive ideas and falsely suggest that their status was equal to that of the colonizers. In Indonesia, natives were forbidden to use the Dutch language whenever colonial rulers wished to underscore the racist caste system symbolically, even though Dutch was otherwise taught in high school. Settlers in particular tended to keep the education of the natives minimal and restricted to local languages. The issue was often resolved by the fact that only missionaries would bother to learn "native languages" in order to teach in those languages or to train future catechists and teachers. Traditional forms of instruction, such as Koran schools, were sometimes suppressed (Algeria) and sometimes unaltered (Malaya). Wherever education for the village population was propagated, only practical agricultural information, knowledge of the Bible, and elementary modern technology were considered appropriate subjects for the curriculum. The basic idea was that the horizon of the rural child was limited to the village and should remain so.

Behind the language problem lurked the question of the educational value of the native tradition. At least in theory, France early on emphasized the primacy of the French tradition in a kind of cultural chauvinism, under the catchword of "assimilation," but later occasionally introduced some degree of educational diversity. The *lycées* of Hanoi and Saigon, in which a minority of Vietnamese were instructed side by side with French, even allowed classical Chinese to be substituted for Latin and Greek. In the early nineteenth century, a major debate unfolded in India between the romantic friends of native culture, the "Orientalists," and the group of "Anglicists," who were influenced by anti-romantic utilitarianism. The fact that English prevailed in higher education and as a medium of public communication was certainly an expression of European cultural hegemony. However, the use of English was not merely a colonialist imposition. Among the Indians there was a growing general demand for European education, not only as a prerequisite for a career in the public service. Toward the end of the nineteenth century, the demand had become strong enough to support a prospering private school system in the big cities.

In the Philippines, the American conquerors responded to a vigorous demand for educational opportunities with ambitious programs. Departing from the usual reserved caution of colonial rulers, they aspired by means of cultural assimilation to encourage ties to America not only by the elite, but also by the indigenous masses. No other colonial power made a greater priority of national education than the United States. In 1939, one quarter of the Philippine population could speak English, in stark contrast to the situation in Indonesia in 1930, where a mere 0.32 percent of the total population could read Dutch, despite significant educational efforts since the early years of the twentieth century.[164] In parts of Africa, there was already a strong desire for education, for example among the Fanti on the Gold Coast, who had developed plans for a western-style public educational system even *before* colonial occupation.[165] European knowledge and its dissemination thus held an attraction quite *early* for small groups outside Europe—even in as self-contained a society as Japan. This attraction cannot be explained directly by a colonial system of domination. In the *late* colonial period, the disproportion between educational expectations and the means to meet them, which were limited both quantitatively and qualitatively, proved to be a further reason for dissatisfaction with the colonial system.

Established colonial pedagogy was invariably disdainful of indigenous cultures. Missionaries and other teachers usually showed little interest in imparting knowledge of local cultures. The famous reproach that young Algerians and Annamites were required to learn senseless lessons about "our ancestors, the Gauls," however, cuts two ways. It can be understood as an indictment of narrow-minded cultural imperialism, but also—and this was its original import—as a warning not to strain the limited intelligence of "the lower races." Asians and Africans were generally unable to campaign for curricular inclusion of their own history and literary canon until they had achieved independence. Their campaign represented a reaction to the arrogance of certain western scholars as well as a desire to create historical national myths for both therapeutic and manipulative purposes. Attempts at imbuing young nations with a sense of national identity can never entirely avoid at least a degree of artificiality, as can also be seen from ample nineteenth-century European examples.

The issue of *language* mattered more to the average person and was also politically more explosive than investing history with meaning. Language was used as a political tool to forge an identity. The more fragmented the linguistic landscape in regional and social respects, the more important this tool became. With the support of the American colonial power, the regional language Tagalog was introduced in 1939 as the national language in the Philippines, a very complex archipelago both ethnically and linguistically.[166] This step anticipated a key political move in many other countries after independence. Under far less magnanimous French rule in Vietnam, the project of recording and modernizing the colloquial language spoken by more than four fifths of the population was a cultural-political undertaking that brought together nationalists and "collaborators." This project, which began in about 1920, paved the way for a common communicative basis in creating a nation.[167] When there was no language comprehensible to the majority, as was the case in India and in large parts of Africa, even nationalist activists clung to the idiom of the colonial rulers. The universal use of English created a basis for coordination of the Indian struggle for freedom across the whole subcontinent. It permitted "two Indians to talk to each other in a tongue which neither party hates."[168]

Colonial culture was (and post-colonial culture continues to be) caught in a tension between the affirmation of indigenous culture and the adoption of foreign culture. Colonialism had begun by destroying old traditions or throwing them off balance, but after only two or three generations it unintentionally produced its own independent cultural offerings. The languages of the colonizers evolved into a means of criticizing colonialism. Garcilaso de la Vega, a Christian whose primary residence was in Spain and who was descended from the royal family of the Incas on his mother's side, crafted an important work of historiography with his *Comentarios reales de los Incas* (1609), written in the loftiest humanist Spanish. This book did not openly condemn the Spanish conquest, but certainly shifted it into a critical light by invoking the splendors of old Peru. Some of the most effective critiques of colonialism in later centuries were also written by non-European authors directly in the languages of the colonizers.

In the New World, Spanish, Portuguese, English, and French so overwhelmed the linguistic landscape that indigenous idioms could not flourish. By contrast, in Asia and later in Africa, a dual process of appropriating the imported language *and* renewing awareness of traditional modes of expression took place concurrently. Sometimes this dual process converged in a single individual. The great Bengali writer Rabindranath Tagore, who was awarded the Nobel Prize for Literature in 1913, translated some of his works into English himself; his famous novel *The Home and the World* (1910) even appeared in print in the English language six years before the original version in Bengali. Kenya's most famous writer, Ngugi wa Thiong'o, composes his works in English as well as in Kikuyu and Swahili. Other authors, especially Indian and African authors, have opted for English or French altogether and have created works of world literature in these languages. Salman Rushdie sees no further sense in the post-colonial debate on the pros and cons of using English in India: "What seems to me to be happening is that those peoples who were once colonized by the [English] language are now rapidly remaking it, domesticating it, becoming more and more relaxed about the way they use it . . . The children of independent India seem not to think of English as being irredeemably tainted by its colonial provenance. They use it as an Indian language, as one of the tools they have to hand."[169]

Colonialist Ideology

The White Man's Burden
(Literary Digest 18; February 18, 1899)

In contrast to other "isms," colonialism is extremely difficult to place in the history of thought. Ever since the major debate on the meaning of America in Spanish Late Scholasticism,[170] all colonialisms have produced a variety of doctrines of justification and imperial visions. However, they have seldom been recognized as binding principles and actually been put into practice. Well-known programs such as British "indirect rule" and French "assimilation" were never realized quite in the sense of their creators. They remained utopias of a well-ordered colonialism. Rather than seeking out contemporary "theories," scholars would be better advised to cast a wider net by inquiring into the mentalities that were associated with the colonial situation. The latest research enjoys using the term "colonial discourse," which it investigates in a large palette of source material: missionary reports and administrative files, memoirs, travel accounts and fictional literature, the press, propaganda pieces, and academic investigations from many fields including geography, ethnology, and oriental philology.[171]

Only by risking extreme oversimplification can we generalize about the views of the colonizers across place, time, and national-cultural attitudes. Two additional complications bear mention. For one, not all "whites" in a colony were also colonial *rulers*. In an influential analysis of colonialism, the Tunisian writer Albert Memmi pointed out in 1957 that not every "colonizer" became a "colonialist"; there was also the "colonizer with good intentions," who tried to avoid crass exercise of power or who even fought against the colonial system.[172] One example is the writer George Orwell. Between 1922 and 1927, Orwell was a police officer in Burma. Orwell gave literary expression to his experiences in several texts that were sharply critical of colonialism (especially "Burmese Days," "Shooting an Elephant," and "A Hanging"). For another, an important psychological aspect of the colonial situation has been noted by the writer Aimé Césaire and the psychoanalyst Oscar Mannoni: in a master-servant relationship marked by ethnic difference, the masters also suffer deformations of their personalities and are dehumanized.[173] Seen in this light, statements by colonizers should be analyzed not only as expressions of ideology, but also as social pathology.

These differentiations notwithstanding, three basic elements of colonialist thought may be identified: the notion of irreconcilable difference, a belief in the higher consecration of colonization, and the utopian vision of a purifying administration that obliterates all corruption and inefficiency.

1) *Anthropological counterparts: the construction of inferior "otherness."* The notion that non-Europeans differ utterly and essentially from Europeans was a cornerstone of colonialist thought. The inferior mental and physical abilities imputed to non-Europeans would render them incapable of the large-scale cultural accomplishments and heroic deeds that only modern Europe could achieve. This principal assumption of difference was elaborated in various ways. Theologically, difference was explained as the depravity of heathens. Technologically, difference was evident to Europeans in the allegedly inferior ability of non-Europeans to control nature. Environmentally, residents of the tropics were supposedly compromised by a climate that weakened their bodily constitutions. Biologically, non-Europeans were said to differ from Europeans in a set of inalterable racial characteristics. The predominant ideas in a given situation historically followed roughly this order of importance. Racism was the ultimate version of the difference axiom. At least in the three or four decades before World War I, it was unquestioningly accepted by Europeans and Americans of nearly all political persuasions.

Of course, it is far from clear what is to be understood by "racism" in its historically evolving meaning and in scholarly opinion. Gilbert Murray, the English scholar of antiquity, famous in his time as a liberal and humanist, formulated the core of racial thought in 1900 with surprisingly emphatic agreement: "There is in the world a hierarchy of races ... those nations which eat more, claim more, and get higher wages, will direct and rule the others, and the lower work of the world will tend in the long-run to be done by the lower breeds of men. This much we of the ruling colour will no doubt accept as obvious."[174] Murray's statement goes to the heart of racist thought, since he establishes a constitutive connection with the exploitation of the work force for almost all racism, with the exception of anti-semitism.[175] This line of thought met with general approval and seemed irrefutably corroborated by biology and anthropology. However, not all colonial practitioners transformed racist theory into violent practice. If we seek a more general consensus for colonialist thought in its late phase after 1920, when straightforward biological determinism gradually fell out of favor in scholarship, we find the notion (still widespread today) that there is an African, Oriental, Indian (or whatever collective unit is chosen) *character*, which disqualifies non-Europeans from association with Europeans on an equal footing. The lay psychology of colonial expatriates, applied on an everyday basis and continually reaffirmed by the mechanism of the self-fulfilling prophecy, was based on a series of characterological generalizations: the "natives" were said to be lazy, shiftless, cruel, playful, naive, dissolute, duplicitous, incapable of abstract thought, impulsive, etc.[176] However, serious scholarship has also operated with judgmental antitheses. So-called Orientalism is based on the mental operation of distancing inversion, in which "the Orient" is held to be the antithesis of Europe in every respect—static, lacking history, incapable of self-reflection, etc.[177] The long-influential theory of the "dual economy" claimed the co-existence of a sluggish, traditional subsistence sector and a dynamic, modern export sector under management from abroad. The early writings in this vein proceeded from a set of simplistic economic and anthropological assumptions concerning the attitudes of native producers. The Asian was said not to be a "homo oeconomicus" and might have to be coaxed into diligent prosperity.

2) *Belief in mission and guardianship.* The axiom of difference dictates that those who are dependent or immature by nature are in need of guidance. This guidance automatically falls to those highest in the pecking order of races and civilizations. Legitimation of colonial rule in the nineteenth and twentieth centuries until the League of Nations concept of mandate was based not on the *right* of the conqueror to rule, but on the claim that conquerors were fulfilling a universal historical mission as liberators from tyranny and spiritual gloom.[178] Rulers claimed two moral *duties*: to bring the blessings of western civilization to the inhabitants of the tropics and to activate neglected resources in backward countries for

the general benefit of the world economy. Lord Lugard formulated this claim in 1922 in his famous theory of the "dual mandate." Guardianship by developed nations or "higher races," in the view of Lugard and others, was said to be essential in all areas: politically, since the Africans were allegedly incapable of self-rule and the Asians needed gradual weaning from their despotic traditions, economically, since work ethics and basic economic skills would have to be instilled in the populace, and culturally, since Africans and Asians would be incapable of freeing themselves from their usual bad habits, "superstitious" ideas, and misguided moral behavior on their own initiative and insight. This view presupposed a complementary rather than an exploitative relationship between colonized and colonizers, since each side required the other. Time and again the "responsibility" of the higher-status minority of the world's population toward the underdeveloped majority was stressed ("the white man's burden"). Colonial rule was glorified as the gift and act of grace of civilization, and was respected as humanitarian intervention. The burden of this task was said to be so enormous that rapid accomplishment of it would be unthinkable. Even the most liberal European representatives of benevolent educational colonialism imagined it was permanent right up to the moment of decolonization. This perception was of relatively recent origin; until at least the mid-nineteenth century, many political elites in the colonized countries did not anticipate sustained rule over "colored" peoples.

3) *Utopia of Non-Politics*

Justifications of the colonial project as a civilizing mission began with the Iberian annexation of territory, escalated between about 1880 and 1914, and entered a final phase, in which the rhetoric shifted from "guardianship" to "trusteeship," after World War I. In this final phase, quite a few writers on colonial affairs harbored dreams of a cultural synthesis of East and West. The colonialist utopia of an administration free of politics remained a constant through the ages. The Europeans believed they had uncovered "chaos" onto which they had to impose order. This order was never quite secure; the Europeans feared that the suppressed anarchy and instinctive nature of their wards was never entirely in check. Both settlers and high bureaucrats were plagued by their dread of chaos, imagining that a single moment of weakness would encourage troublemakers to provoke a "black rebellion."[179]

Even *before* the actual colonization, the establishment of order began with a process of naming and classifying: "By putting regions on a map and native words on a list, explorers laid the first, and deepest, foundations for colonial power."[180] The organizational restoration and configuration began with an elimination of misappropriations, then turned to the art of bureaucratic geometry, without regard for the tumult in the parties and special interest advocates. This process typified the structural reorganization of the exploitation colonies. In the settlement colonies, the obvious rivalry between colonists and indigenous people restricted administrative maneuvers.

A key to success of the great European proconsuls was their tendency "to depoliticize politics and reduce all human affairs to questions of proper administration," as Lord Cromer, the highest authority in Egypt between 1883 and 1906, has been described.[181] In his *Modern Egypt* (1908), a comprehensive account of British colonial thought in the age of high imperialism, Cromer often referred to Egypt's government as a "machine" that was kept in motion by imperial will alone. For this reason, the colonial state reacted with irritation and reluctance to even harmless and loyal attempts to introduce western forms of politics. Nothing was to ruffle the calm of efficient administration. Complaints about "the crushing load of boredom"[182] surfaced repeatedly in testimonials of colonized people in societies in which a return to traditional forms of politics was cut off and access to modern politics was also denied. Many were attracted to nationalist movements in the hope of overcoming their political paralysis.

The notion that colonialist thought was restricted to the colonizers is just as misguided as the view that all criticism came from the victims of the system. European stereotypes of other cultures were often absorbed into the thought patterns of these cultures through education, habit, lack of alternatives, and identification with the aggressor. Many Indians, for instance, either accepted the British prejudice that they were "weak" by nature or sought to refute it with overzealous participation in sports and other masculine rites of passage.[183] A feeling of inadequacy inheres in the basic mental outlook of every colonized people. In the westernized milieus of the colonial world, it was especially evident that heroic efforts to master European culture still failed to yield full recognition by members of the "imperial race." Inevitably, however, there came the historic moment in which a hitherto weak and dependent group of educated inhabitants of a colonial society broke the spell and took up the fight for cultural hegemony. From then on, reinforced, revived, or invented native traditions were cultivated in opposition to colonialist thought. Moreover, the philosophical, juridical, and aesthetic ideas of Europe were turned against colonialism, with devastating effect.

Decolonization

I have entrusted to my Uncle the duty of acting as my representative at the celebrations of the Independence of your country. This is a great and memorable day for you; my thoughts and my good wishes are with you as you take up the great and stimulating responsibilities of independence; and it is with deep and real pleasure that I welcome you to the brotherhood of our Commonwealth family of nations. I am confident that Malaya will respond worthily to the challenging tasks of independence, and that she will continue to show to the world that example of co-operation and goodwill between all races that has been so marked a feature of her history. May God bless you and guide your country in the years that lie ahead.

31st August, 1957.

*Queen Elizabeth II's letter in celebration
of the Independence of Malaysia*

The decolonization of Asia, Africa, and the Caribbean has apparently reached an end.[184] The ceremonial handing over of government affairs to leaders of the new nations is now a thing of the past. The inauguration of Zimbabwe, the former Rhodesia, on April 17, 1980 may have been the final expression of exuberance at a new beginning that characterized many transfers of power after World War II. Today even the great programmatic designs of Afro-Asiatic emancipation seem to have receded into history. With the sole exception of the theology of "liberation" and economic theory of "dependencia" in Latin America in the 1960s and 1970s,[185] the South never again challenged the West with the depth and precision of focus found in the now-classic anti-imperialist teachings and polemics of Gandhi and Jawaharlal Nehru, Mao Zedong and Ho Chi Minh, Jamal al-din al-Afgani and Frantz Fanon, Kwame Nkrumah and Léopold Sédar Senghor.[186]

Each colonial situation experienced its end and transition to a post-colonial state of affairs in its own distinctive way. Historical analysis of individual cases must take an extensive assortment of factors into account. At least *six dimensions* need to be considered: 1) the societal and economic circumstances in the colony; 2) leadership, goals, forms of action, mass support, and strength of the anti-colonial liberation movements; 3) the willingness of colonial regimes and settlers to use force; 4) colonial economic interests and colonial political decisions in the metropolises; 5) the influence of third powers (especially of the United States and the Soviet Union); and 6) world economic constellations.

The *third* phase of the withdrawal of colonial rule[187] restructured the international system. World War II had hit the European colonial empires hard, but did not directly bring about their collapse. The British, French, and Dutch, with the aid of the Americans, were quickly at hand in Asia to fill the vacuum created by the breakdown of the Japanese military empire;

the European position in Africa and the Middle East did not seem endangered anyway. In 1946, the political world map was still contoured almost exactly as it had been at the height of the European domination of the world. Based on the resources and prestige of their immense empires, the British and, to a lesser extent, the French laid claim to equality in world politics with the main victors of the World War, the United States and the Soviet Union.

Only two decades later, the French colonial empire had virtually ceased to exist. Charles de Gaulle centered French politics firmly on Europe.[188] The British retreat proceeded at a slower pace; it was driven far less by national wars of liberation than the French retreat.[189] However, within two decades of the independence and partition of India in 1947, the British retreat was essentially complete. Economic frailty in the imperial center was a crucial factor. A crippling weakness in the British economy was revealed in the sterling crisis of November 1967, ironically under a Labour government that was dedicated to maintaining both the Empire and a high profile in world politics.[190] From then on, the last Empire enthusiasts relinquished the idea of an imperial Britain. When the United Kingdom joined the European Community in 1973, the end of British orientation overseas was signalled. Holland had already left Indonesia in 1949; the Belgians had fled their Congo colony in 1960. Only Portugal was able to maintain its "third" overseas empire (after the short-lived mercantile empire in Asia and the more stable presence in Brazil) until 1975.[191]

As an aspect of international politics, decolonization helped effect a transition to a new world order. Until the great upheaval of the years 1989-1991, this new order was characterized by: 1) global confrontations of two highly armed blocs, 2) the re-Europeanization of the (West) European great powers, 3) the emergence of numerous post-colonial new nations, which generally entered into patron-client relations with either the United States or the Soviet Union, 4) strengthening of international organizations, especially the United Nations, in comparison to the period preceding 1945, and 5) a widespread ideological denunciation of colonialism, although in practice racial discrimination did not entirely disappear in international relations.[192]

Economic decolonization must be seen as the outgrowth of *political* decolonization. The post-colonial nations were essentially sovereign in the economic sphere. They could now determine their own currencies, finances, and legal systems, and, if they wished, eliminate the key foreign positions in the domestic economy—in extreme cases by expropriating foreign firms and expelling settlers. The fact that this rarely occurred to the fullest extent, as it did in Algeria, is a different matter. Being one's own boss was a long way from liberation from the networks and dependencies of the world economy that had been built up in lengthy processes. Not a single post-colonial state possessed the conditions for "auto-centered" development independent of international entanglements. As soon as political freedom for economic action was attained, each of the post-colonial governments therefore found itself caught between nationalist self-isolation and humble acceptance of peripheral market opportunities, often by intercession of multinational concerns and international economic organizations. Decolonization gave the ex-colonies freedom of action, but seldom the opportunity to exploit it to full advantage.

If colonialism is understood to be a reciprocal relationship, *decolonization of the colonizers* must have occurred as well. Only in France was this process *politically* agonizing, since the political system of the Fourth Republic was badly shaken by the war in Indochina and destroyed by the war in Algeria in 1958. British settlers, lobbyists, and colonial officers had had far less influence than the French over domestic politics in the colonies. Decisions concerning the British Empire were carried out by a consensus of the leading parties in London within a stable parliamentary system.[193]

Economically, the European colonial powers coped with the loss of their empires better than two groups had predicted, namely the defenders of the colonial status quo and the proponents of the theory that colonial exploitation was vital for capitalist economies. The relative weakness of the British postwar economy had contributed substantially to loosening the British grip on the Empire. However, England's economic woes were not primarily induced by the erosion of colonial ties. France had a much greater cause for concern as decolonization escalated, since the imperial collapse in North Africa and Indochina necessitated the repatriation of over 1.5 million overseas French within a few short years.[194] The anticipated problems did not materialize, however. After all earlier colonial powers, even the latecomer Portugal, had succeeded in reorienting their policies from late colonial neo-mercantilism to European-Atlantic free trade, the empires began to seem more like burdens that had been cast off just in time than objects of nostalgic idealization.

The end of overseas colonial empires did not eliminate all circumstances to which the definition of colonialism could apply. Concepts of colonialism and decolonization might further our understanding of the multicultural Soviet Union and neighboring satellite nations that were under its military control. This area has not been addressed in sufficient detail and goes beyond the scope of the present study; it presents great challenges to theories of comparative colonialism and imperialism.[195] The most obvious cases of colonial rule in the 1990s are no longer in the residual European area of control, but within the "Third World." In Tibet, China practices a virtually flawless colonial politics right down to invasions by settlers and a justification of a "civilizing mission" on the basis of historically dubious claims.[196] Indonesian rule in East Timor, which replaced a centuries-old Portuguese regiment over the protest of the United Nations Security Council in 1975,[197] the somewhat less brutal politics of Morocco in the Western Sahara, and, until recently, the areas occupied by Israel in 1967 with a Palestinian population majority[198] all have characteristics of colonialism without being fully developed systems of colonial rule.

Conversely, the last European and United States overseas possessions, which number just over forty, seldom arouse criticism of colonialism. Hong Kong, cosmopolitan city and center of growth *par excellence*, was ruled as a British Crown Colony in an old-fashioned, liberal, and undemocratic manner. It is no longer the colonial power, but the People's Republic of China that has sabotaged any enlargement of political participation before the 1997 merger with the mother country. The population of Hong Kong has no guarantee that its average standard of living will be maintained.[199] The French *départements* and *territoires d'outre-mer* (Guadeloupe, Martinique, Réunion, New Caledonia, and others) are more closely tied to the structures of the metropolises than is the case with Hong Kong. The "DOM-TOMs" receive considerable subsidies from the treasury in Paris, their approximately 1.5 million citizens enjoy all political and civil rights of the French, settle in France as they please, and benefit from most services of the French welfare state. In contrast to the case of Hong Kong, no change of status is likely. The majority of the French people reject any change with frankly nationalist arguments; the overseas beneficiaries of the "subsidised consumer economy"[200] show little interest in independence.

Colonialism as a form of European world rule completed its historical cycle in the third quarter of the twentieth century. Although the current crisis in the southern hemisphere, particularly in the African continent, cannot be blamed wholly on European colonial rule, and the particular attribution of cause and effect is often extremely difficult, the effects of colonization, whether positive or negative, are ubiquitous. The post-colonial world has retained forms of manipulation, exploitation, and cultural expropriation, even if colonialism itself belongs to the past.

Notes

1 See Otto Brunner, Werner Conze, and Reinhart Koselleck, eds., *Geschichtliche Grundbegriffe. Historisches Lexikon zur politisch-sozialen Sprache in Deutschland* (Stuttgart: Klett-Cotta, 1972-92). However, vol. III (1982) contains an article on "Imperialism" by Jörg Fisch, Dieter Groh, and Rudolf Walther (pp. 171-236).

2 Moses I. Finley, "Colonies: An Attempt at a Typology," in *Transactions of the Royal Historical Society*, 5th ser., 26 (1976), pp. 167-188.

3 See, for example, William Y. Adams, "The First Colonial Empire: Egypt in Nubia, 3200-1200 B.C.," in *Comparative Studies in Society and History*, 26 (1984), pp. 36-71; Joshua Prawer, *The Crusaders' Kingdom: European Colonialism in the Middle Ages* (New York: Praeger, 1972).

4 *Duden. Fremdwörterbuch*, 3rd ed. (Mannheim: Dudenverlag, 1974), p. 381.

5 Henri Brunschwig, *Noirs et blancs dans l'Afrique noire française* (Paris: Flammarion, 1983), p. 209. Emphasis added.

6 See the theoretical definition in John J. McCusker and Russell R. Menard, *The Economy of British America, 1607-1789* (Chapel Hill: Univ. of North Carolina Press, 1985), p. 21.

7 See Steven G. Marks, *Road to Power: The Trans-Siberian Railroad and the Colonization of Asian Russia, 1850-1917* (Ithaca: Cornell Univ. Press, 1991), pp. 196 ff.

8 See Francis Bacon, "Of Plantations" [1625], in *The Essays*, ed. John Pitcher (Harmondsworth: Penguin, 1985), pp. 162-164.

9 See Paul Mosley, *The Settler Economies: Studies in the Economic History of Kenya and Southern Rhodesia, 1900-1963* (Cambridge: Cambridge Univ. Press, 1983), pp. 5-8, 237 (fn. 1).

10 Robert William Fogel, *Without Consent or Contract: The Rise and Fall of American Slavery* (New York: Norton, 1989), pp. 30 f.

11 Mark A. Burkholder and Lyman L. Johnson, *Colonial Latin America* (New York & Oxford: Oxford Univ. Press, 1990), p. 106.

12 Paul S. Reinsch, *Colonial Government: An Introduction to the Study of Colonial Institutions* (New York: Macmillan, 1902), p. 16.

13 On the particular type of harbor colony, it is still useful to refer to Ernst Grünfeld, *Hafenkolonien und kolonieähnliche Verhältnisse in China, Japan und Korea* (Jena: Gustav Fischer, 1913).

14 Philip D. Curtin, "The Black Experience of Colonialism and Imperialism," in Sidney W. Mintz, ed., *Slavery, Colonialism, and Racism* (New York: Norton, 1974), p. 23.

15 I follow Michael Winter, *Egyptian Society under Ottoman Rule 1517-1798* (London & New York: Routledge, 1992), p. 30.

16 Edward W. Said, *Culture and Imperialism* (New York: Knopf, 1993), p. 9.

17 Philip Mason, *Patterns of Dominance* (London: Oxford Univ. Press, 1970), p. 274.

18 For an overview with critical commentary, see Robert J. Hind, "The Internal Colonial Concept," in *Comparative Studies in Society and History,* 26 (1984), pp. 543-568. It probably makes more sense to speak of "internal periphery"; see Hans-Heinrich Nolte, ed. *Internal Peripheries in European History* (Göttingen: Musterschmidt Verlag, 1991).

19 The English historians Ronald E. Robinson and John A. Gallagher set the basis for these distinctions. See especially Wm. Roger Louis, ed., *Imperialism: The Robinson and Gallagher Controversy* (New York: New Viewpoints, 1976); R. E. Robinson, "The Excentric Idea of Empire—with or without Imperialism," in Wolfgang J. Mommsen & Jürgen Osterhammel, eds., *Imperialism and After: Continuities and Discontinuities* (London & Boston: Allen & Unwin, 1986), pp. 267-289. See also the important continuation of this line of thought in Michael W. Doyle, *Empires* (Ithaca & London: Cornell Univ. Press, 1986), pp. 19-47.

20 See the following complementary volumes: Ramon H. Myers and Mark R. Peattie, eds., *The Japanese Colonial Empire, 1895-1945* (Princeton: Princeton Univ. Press, 1984) and Peter Duus et al., eds, *The Japanese Informal Empire in China, 1895-1937* (Princeton Univ. Press, 1989). William G. Beasley provides an exemplary overview in *Japanese Imperialism 1894-1945* (Oxford & New York: Oxford Univ. Press, 1987).

21 See J. van Goor, "Imperialisme in de marge?" in J. van Goor, ed., *Imperialisme in de marge: De afronding van Nederlands-Indi'* (Utrecht: HES Uitgevers, 1986), p. 9. But for an earlier period, see Maarten Kuitenbrouwer, *The Netherlands and the Rise of Modern Imperialism: Colonies and Foreign Policies, 1870-1902* (New York: Berg Publishers, 1991).

22 Most of the developments discussed here are thoroughly described and analyzed in a work by Wolfgang Reinhard, which remains unsurpassed in any language: *Geschichte der europäischen Expansion*, 4 vols. (Stuttgart: Kohlhammer, 1983-1990). A fine introduction to imperialism as a theoretical issue is Andrew Porter, *European Imperialism, 1860-1914* (Basingstoke & London: Macmillan, 1994).

23 Arthur Girault, *Principes de colonisation et de législation coloniale*, I, 4th ed. (Paris: Larose, 1921), p. 17.

24 David Lowenthal, *West Indian Societies* (New York: Oxford Univ. Press, 1972), p. 29.

25 J. S. Furnivall, *Colonial Policy and Practice: A Comparative Study of Burma and Netherlands India* (Cambridge, England: Cambridge Univ. Press, 1948), p. 5.

26 See the classic essay by Georges Balandier, "La situation coloniale: Approche théoretique," in *Cahiers internationaux de sociologie*, 10/11 (1951), pp. 44-79.

27 See Paul Carter, *The Road to Botany Bay: An Exploration of Landscape and History* (New York: Knopf, 1988), p. xvi.

28 J. F. A. Ajayi, "Colonialism: An Episode in African History" in Lewis H. Gann & Peter Duignan, eds., *Colonialism in Africa 1870-1960*, I (Cambridge: Cambridge Univ. Press, 1969), p. 505.

29 Clifford Geertz uses this example in *Islam Observed: Religious Development in Morocco and Indonesia* (New Haven: Yale Univ. Press, 1968), pp. 62-65.

30 Adam Smith, *An Inquiry into the Nature and Causes of the Wealth of Nations*, ed. R. H. Campbell and A.S. Skinner (Oxford: Clarendon Press, 1976), II, 564.

31 J. H. Elliott, *Spain and its World 1500-1700: Selected Essays* (New Haven: Yale Univ. Press, 1989), p. 13.

32 Elliott, p. 15.

33 Immanuel Wallerstein, *Capitalist Agriculture and the Origins of the European World-Economy in the 16th Century*, Vol. I of *The Modern World-System* (New York: Academic Press, 1974), p. 336.

34 The definitive study is by J. H. Galloway: *The Sugar Cane Industry: An Historical Geography from its Origins to 1914* (New York: Cambridge Univ. Press, 1989). More relevant as cultural than as economic history is Sidney W. Mintz, *Sweetness and Power: The Place of Sugar in Modern History* (New York: Viking, 1985).

35 These statistics are from Philip D. Curtin, *The Atlantic Slave Trade: A Census* (Madison: Univ. of Wisconsin Press, 1969), p. 268 (table 77).

36 See John E. McClellan, *Colonialism and Science: Saint Domingue in the Old Regime* (Baltimore: Johns Hopkins Univ. Press, 1992), p. 2.

37 See John Brewer, *The Sinews of Power: War, Money, and the English State, 1688-1783* (Boston: Unwin Hyman, 1989); Lawrence Stone, ed., *An Imperial State at War: Britain from 1689 to 1815* (London & New York; Routledge, 1994); P. J. Cain & A. G. Hopkins, *British Imperialism: Innovation and Expansion, 1688-1914* (London & New York: Longman, 1993), I, 71-84.

38 Quoted in Percival Spear, *Master of Bengal: Clive and his India* (London: Thames and Hudson, 1975), p.146. On early British expansion in India, see P. J. Marshall, *Bengal: The British Bridgehead. Eastern India 1740-1828* (Cambridge: Cambridge Univ. Press, 1987).

39 Gordon K. Lewis, *The Growth of the Modern West Indies* (New York: Monthly Review Press, 1968), p. 63.

40 For an exhaustive treatment of this topic using the example of China, see

124 COLONIALISM: A THEORETICAL OVERVIEW

Jürgen Osterhammel, *China und die Weltgesellschaft. Vom 18. Jahrhundert bis in unsere Zeit* (Munich: C.H. Beck, 1989), pp. 139-201.

41 These figures are from John Ruedy, *Modern Algeria: The Origins and Development of a Nation* (Bloomington: Indiana Univ. Press, 1992), p. 69 (table 3.1) and Jörg Fisch, *Geschichte Südafrikas* (Munich: Deutscher Taschenbuch Verlag, 1990), p. 144.

42 See H. L.Wesseling, *Verdeel en heers: De deling van Afrika 1880-1914* (Amsterdam: Bert Bakker, 1992), p. 18.

43 Roland Oliver, *The African Experience* (London: Weidenfeld & Nicolson, 1991), p. 184.

44 Article 22, para. 1 of the Covenant of the League of Nations of 1919; in Ruth B. Henig, ed., *The League of Nations* (Edinburgh: Oliver and Boyd, 1973), p. 186.

45 See Wm. Roger Louis, "The Era of the Mandates System and the Non-European World," in Hedley Bull & Adam Watson, eds., *The Expansion of International Society* (Oxford: Clarendon Press & Oxford Univ. Press, 1984), pp. 201-213.

46 See Phillip Darby, *Three Faces of Imperialism: British and American Approaches to Asia and Africa 1870-1970* (New Haven: Yale Univ. Press, 1987), pp. 84 f.

47 See the major study of Philip S. Khoury, *Syria and the French Mandate. The Politics of Arab Nationalism, 1920-1945* (Princeton: Princeton Univ. Press, 1987), esp. pp. 27-94.

48 See David E. Omissi, *Air Power and Colonial Control: The Royal Air Force 1919-1939* (Manchester & New York: Manchester Univ. Press, 1990).

49 Ample material on this subject can be found in Rudolf von Albertini's panoramic *European Colonial Rule, 1880-1940. The Impact of the West on India, Southeast Asia, and Africa* (Oxford: Clio Press, 1982).

50 See Reinhard, *Geschichte der europäischen Expansion* (as in fn. 22), II, 203 f.

51 W. David McIntyre, *The Significance of the Commonwealth, 1965-1990,* (Basingstoke: Macmillan, 1991), p. 15.

52 John D. Hargreaves, *Decolonization in Africa* (London & New York: Longman, 1988), p. 108; D.A. Low, *Eclipse of Empire* (Cambridge & New York: Cambridge Univ. Press, 1991), pp. 173-176.

53 See David K. Fieldhouse, *Black Africa, 1945-1980: Economic Decolonization and Arrested Development* (London: Allen & Unwin, 1986), p. 23.

54 D.W. Meinig, *Atlantic America, 1492-1800,* Vol. I of *The Shaping of America: A Geographical Perspective on 500 Years of History* (New Haven: Yale Univ. Press, 1986), pp. 65 f.

55 See John H. Elliott, "The Seizure of Overseas Territories by the European Powers," in Hans Pohl, ed., *The European Discovery of the World and its*

Economic Effects on Pre-Industrial Society, 1500-1800 (Stuttgart: F. Steiner, 1990), pp. 51-54.

56 John Iliffe, *A Modern History of Tanganyika* (Cambridge & New York: Cambridge Univ. Press, 1979), p. 117.

57 David Geggus, "The Haitian Revolution" in Franklin W. Knight and Colin A. Palmer, eds, *The Modern Caribbean* (Chapel Hill: Univ. of North Carolina Press, 1989), p. 39; Y. G. Paillard, "The French Expedition to Madagascar in 1895: Program and Results," in J. A. de Moor & H. L. Wesseling, eds., *Imperialism and War: Essays on Colonial Wars in Asia and Africa* (Leiden: Leiden Univ. Press, 1989), pp.183 f.

58 Quoted from John M. MacKenzie's introduction to the volume he edited: *Popular Imperialism and the Military 1850-1950* (Manchester & New York: Manchester Univ. Press, 1992), p. 7.

59 See Inga Clendinnen, *The Aztecs: An Interpretation* (Cambridge & New York: Cambridge Univ. Press, 1991), pp. 267-273.

60 P. M. Holt & M. W. Daly, *A History of the Sudan*, 4th ed. (London & New York, 1988), p. 112.

61 See Tzvetan Todorov, *The Conquest of America: The Question of the Other*, trans. Richard Howard (New York: HarperCollins, 1987), pp. 51-123; but compare the contradictory conclusions of Inga Clendinnen, "'Fierce and Unnatural Cruelty': Cortés and the Conquest of Mexico," in Stephen Greenblatt, ed., *New World Encounters* (Berkeley: Univ. of California Press, 1993), pp. 12-47.

62 See James Belich, *The New Zealand Wars and the Victorian Interpretation of Racial Conflict* (Auckland: Auckland Univ. Press, 1986), pp. 291 ff.

63 See the case study by Stig Förster, *Die mächtigen Diener der East India Company. Ursachen und Hintergründe der britischen Expansionspolitik in Südasien 1793-1819* (Stuttgart: F. Steiner, 1992).

64 For an overview of this research, see Catherine Coquery-Vidrovitch, *Africa: Endurance and Change South of the Sahara,* trans. David Maisel (Berkeley: Univ. of California Press, 1988), pp. 168-210.

65 This is the theory of Michael Adas, "From Avoidance to Confrontation: Peasant Protest in Precolonial and Colonial Southeast Asia," in Nicholas B. Dirks, ed., *Colonialism and Culture* (Ann Arbor: Univ. of Michigan Press, 1992), p. 112.

66 See Charles Gibson, *The Aztecs under Spanish Rule: A History of the Indios of the Valley of Mexico, 1519-1810* (Stanford: Stanford Univ. Press, 1964), p. 404.

67 "[...] doctus per aliena experimenta parum profici armis, si iniuriae sequerentur" Tacitus, *Agricola*, trans. M. Hutton, in: *Tacitus in Five Volumes*, I (Cambridge, Mass.: Harvard Univ. Press, 1970), p. 63.

68 See the definitive study by Michael H. Fisher, *Indirect Rule in India: Resi-*

dents and the Residency System 1764-1858 (New York: Oxford Univ. Press, 1991). For the following period, see Ian Copland, *The British Raj and the Indian Princes: Paramountcy in Western India, 1857-1930* (Bombay: Orient Longman, 1982).

69 See J. M. Gullick, *Rulers and Residents: Influence and Power in the Malay States 1870-1920* (New York: Oxford Univ. Press, 1992).

70 *Report of the Indian Statutory Commission.* Cmd. 3568 (Simon Report), London 1930, p. 112.

71 See William A. Green, *British Slave Emancipation: The Sugar Colonies and the Great Experiment 1830-1865* (Oxford: Clarendon Press, 1976), p. 94.

72 Dane Kennedy, *Islands of White: Settler Society and Culture in Kenya and Southern Rhodesia, 1890-1939* (Durham: Duke Univ. Press, 1987), p. 1.

73 See the comparative overview of G.V. Scammell, *The First Imperial Age: European Overseas Expansion c. 1400-1715* (Boston: Unwin Hyman, 1989), pp. 141-168.

74 See John H. Elliott, "Spain and America before 1700," in Leslie Bethell, ed., *The Cambridge History of Latin America*, I (New York: Cambridge Univ. Press, 1984), p. 74. See also the references to "decentralized patrimonial domination" in Max Weber, *Economy and Society: An Outline of Interpretive Sociology*, ed. Guenther Roth and Claus Wittich, trans. Ephraim Fischoff et al., III (New York: Bedminster Press, 1968), pp. 1051-1055, esp. 1054.

75 See Lisa Anderson, *The State and Social Transformation in Tunisia and Libya, 1830-1980* (Princeton: Princeton Univ. Press, 1986), pp. 185 ff., 251 ff.

76 In a somewhat more circumscribed context, see C. A. Bayly, *Imperial Meridian: The British Empire and the World 1780-1830* (New York: Longman, 1989), pp. 194 ff.

77 See Nancy M. Farriss, *Maya Society under Colonial Rule: The Collective Enterprise of Survival* (Princeton: Princeton Univ. Press, 1984), pp. 355, 366-375.

78 A. D. A. de Kat Angelino, *Le Problème colonial*, I (La Haye: Martinus Nijhoff, 1931), p. 67.

79 See also the Marxist-inspired analysis of Bruce Berman and John Lonsdale, *Unhappy Valley: Conflict in Kenya and Africa*, I (London: J. Currey, 1992), pp. 80 f.

80 See the brilliant analysis in Trutz von Trotha, *Koloniale Herrschaft: Zur soziologischen Theorie der Staatsentstehung am Beispiel des "Schutzgebietes Togo"* (Tübingen: Siebeck, 1994), pp. 86-142.

81 See Clifford Geertz, "The Judging of Nations: Some Comments on the Assessment of Regimes in the New States," in *Archives européennes de sociologie*, 18 (1977), p. 250.

82 See the important case study by David Arnold, *Police Power and Colonial*

Rule: Madras 1859-1947 (New York: Oxford Univ. Press, 1986), esp. pp. 148 and 235.

83 For the British Empire, see David M. Anderson and David Killingray, eds., *Policing and Decolonisation: Politics, Nationalism and the Police, 1917-65* (Manchester & New York: Manchester Univ. Press, 1992).

84 Jörg Fisch, "Law as a Means and as an End: Some Remarks on the Function of European and Non-European Law in the Process of European Expansion," in Wolfgang J. Mommsen and J.A. de Moor, eds., *European Expansion and Law: The Encounter of European and Indigenous Law in 19th and 20th-Century Africa and Asia* (Oxford & New York: Berg, 1991), p. 23.

85 See Chou Whei-ming, *Taiwan unter japanischer Herrschaft 1895-1945* (Bochum: Brockmeyer, 1989), p. 178 f.

86 For an overview, see Kristin Mann and Richard Roberts, "Introduction: Law in Colonial Africa" in Mann and Roberts, eds., *Law in Colonial Africa* (London: James Currey, 1991), pp. 3-58.

87 See Martin J. Murray, *The Development of Capitalism in Colonial Indochina (1870-1940)* (Berkeley: Univ. of California Press, 1980), pp. 21-27.

88 See John Iliffe, *The African Poor: A History* (New York: Cambridge Univ. Press, 1987), p. 171. For background information, see Herward Sieberg, *Colonial Development. Die Grundlegung moderner Entwicklungspolitik durch Großbritannien 1919-1949* (Stuttgart: Steiner, 1985).

89 See Michael Crowder, "The White Chiefs of Tropical Africa," in Lewis H. Gann and Peter Duignan, eds., *Colonialism in Africa, 1870-1960*, II (Cambridge: Cambridge Univ. Press, 1970), p. 324.

90 B. B. Misra, *The Bureaucracy in India: An Historical Account of Development up to 1947* (Delhi: Oxford Univ. Press, 1977), p. 291.

91 See Khasnor Johan, *The Emergence of the Modern Malay Administrative Elite* (New York: Oxford Univ. Press, 1984), pp. 1-5.

92 Andrew C. Nahm, *Korea: Tradition and Transformation. A History of the Korean People* (Elizabeth, NJ: Hollym International Corporation, 1988), pp. 226 and 229.

93 *Report of the Indian Statutory Commission* (as in fn. 70), p. 46. The total population figure is from Dharma Kumar, ed., *The Cambridge Economic History of India*, II (Cambridge: Cambridge Univ. Press, 1982), p. 488 (table 5.7).

94 William Malcolm Hailey, *An African Survey: A Study of the Problems Arising in Africa South of the Sahara* (London & New York: Oxford Univ. Press, 1938), p. 226.

95 The following list was inspired by D. A. Low, *Lion Rampant: Essays on the Study of British Imperialism* (London: Cass, 1973), p. 28; Bernard Cohn, "Representing Authority in Victorian India," in Bernard Cohn, *An Anthropologist Among the Historians and Other Essays* (New York: Oxford Univ.

Press, 1987), pp. 632-682); C. A. Bayly, "Knowing the Country: Empire and Information in India," in *Modern Asian Studies,* 27 (1993), pp.3-43.

96 See the analysis by Edward N. Luttwak, which is illuminating for any political interpretation of imperialism: *The Grand Strategy of the Roman Empire: From the First Century A.D. to the Third* (Baltimore: Johns Hopkins Univ. Press, 1976), pp. 21-40.

97 See P. J. Marshall, *Bengal: The British Bridgehead. Eastern India 1740-1828* (Cambridge: Cambridge Univ. Press, 1987), pp. 120-127. For a comparable study of neighboring Bihar, see Anand A. Yang, *The Limited Raj: Agrarian Relations in Colonial India, Saran District, 1793-1920* (Berkeley: Univ. of California Press, 1989), pp. 70-78, 226 f.

98 See Carl A. Trocki, "Political Structures in the Nineteenth and Early Twentieth Centuries," in Nicholas Tarling, ed., *The Cambridge History of Southeast Asia*, II (Cambridge: Cambridge Univ. Press, 1992), p. 91.

99 See David Gilmartin, *Empire and Islam: Punjab and the Making of Pakistan* (Berkeley: Univ. of California Press, 1988), pp. 18-26.

100 Paul R. Brass, *The Politics of India since Independence*, 2nd ed. (Cambridge & New York: Cambridge Univ. Press, 1994), p. 20.

101 See A. G. Hopkins, *An Economic History of West Africa* (New York: Columbia Univ. Press, 1973), p. 126.

102 See the overview by Catherine Coquery-Vidrovitch, "Les conditions de la dépendance: Histoire du sous-développement," in Catherine Coquery-Vidrovitch and Alain Forest, eds., *Décolonisations et nouvelles dépendances* (Lille: Presses Universitaires de Lille, 1986), pp. 25-48.

103 See, for example, Norman Miners, *Hong Kong under Imperial Rule, 1912-1941* (New York: Oxford Univ. Press, 1987), pp. 207-277.

104 See Catherine Coquery-Vidrovitch et al., *L'Afrique occidentale au temps des français: Colonisateurs et colonisés, c. 1860-1960* (Paris: La Découverte, 1992), pp. 107-110.

105 Daniel R. Headrick, *The Tools of Empire: Technology and European Imperialism in the Nineteenth Century* (New York: Oxford Univ. Press, 1981), p. 181. See also Daniel R. Headrick, *The Tentacles of Progress: Technology Transfer in the Age of Imperialism* (New York: Oxford Univ. Press, 1988), pp. 49-96, as well as the general account by Clarence B. Davis and Kenneth E. Wilburn, Jr., eds, *Railway Imperialism* (New York: Greenwood, 1991).

106 The typology of agrarian forms of enterprise used in the following discussion follows in part the classic essay of Arthur L. Stinchcombe, "Agricultural Enterprise and Rural Class Relations," in *American Journal of Sociology,* 67 (1961-1962), pp. 165-176.

107 See Charles Gibson, "Indian Societies under Spanish Rule," in Leslie Bethell, ed., *The Cambridge History of Latin America*, II (Cambridge & New York: Cambridge Univ. Press, 1984), pp. 403-405.

108 See Hans Werner Tobler, *Die mexikanische Revolution. Gesellschaftlicher*

Wandel und politischer Umbruch, 1876-1940 (Frankfurt: Suhrkamp, 1984), pp. 70 f.

109 Nancy M. Farriss, *Maya Society under Colonial Rule* (as in fn. 77), pp. 366-375 and 382; see also Charles Gibson, *The Aztecs under Spanish Rule* (as in fn. 66), pp. 406 f.

110 On the concept of "peasantisation," see C. A. Bayly, *Indian Society and the Making of the British Empire* (Cambridge: Cambridge Univ. Press, 1988), pp. 136-168, and C. A. Bayly, "Creating a Colonial Peasantry: India and Java c. 1820-1880," in Mushirul Hasan et al., *India and Indonesia from the 1830s to 1914: The Heyday of Colonial Rule* (Leiden & New York: E.J. Brill, 1987), pp. 93-106.

111 Thomas B. Birnberg and Stephen A. Resnick, *Colonial Development; An Econometric Study* (New Haven: Yale Univ. Press, 1975), p. 254.

112 See Pham Cao Duong, *Vietnamese Peasants under French Domination* (Lanham, Md.: Univ. Press of America, 1985), pp. 38-61.

113 Philip D. Curtin, *The Rise and Fall of the Plantation Complex: Essays in Atlantic History* (Cambridge and New York: Cambridge Univ. Press, 1990), pp. 11-13.

114 See Ann Laura Stoler, *Capitalism and Confrontation in Sumatra's Plantation Belt, 1870-1979* (New Haven: Yale Univ. Press, 1985), pp. 14-46, and esp. Jan Breman, *Koelies, planters en koloniale politiek*, 2nd ed. (Dordrecht: Floris Publications, 1987), chs. 3-5.

115 See C. C. Wrigley, "Aspects of Economic History," in Andrew D. Roberts, ed., *The Cambridge History of Africa*, VII (Cambridge: Cambridge Univ. Press, 1986), pp. 108 f.

116 See Ralph A. Austen, *African Economic History: Internal Development and External Dependency* (London: J. Currey, 1987), pp. 173 and 175 f.

117 Reinhard, *Geschichte der europäischen Expansion* (as in fn. 22), IV, 110.

118 See esp. Charles van Onselen, *Studies in the Social and Economic History of the Witwatersrand 1886-1914*, 2 vols. (New York: Longman, 1982).

119 David K. Fieldhouse, *Colonialism 1870-1945: An Introduction* (New York: St. Martin's Press, 1981), pp. 89, 95, 102.

120 For a detailed discussion, see Dietmar Rothermund, *An Economic History of India: From Pre-Colonial Times to 1986* (London: Croom Helm, 1988), pp. 50-65.

121 Korea has thus far proven to be the best testing ground for this thesis. See Dennis L. McNamara, *The Colonial Origins of Korean Enterprise, 1910-1945* (Cambridge & New York: Cambridge Univ. Press, 1990); Carter J. Eckert, *Offspring of Empire: The Koch'ang Kims and the Colonial Origins of Korean Capitalism* (Seattle: University of Washington Press, 1991).

122 A vast literature is devoted to this process. One outstanding discussion is David Hackett Fischer, *Albion's See: Four British Folkways in America*

(New York & Oxford: Oxford Univ. Press, 1989).

123 For a lucid comparison of continental North and South America (excluding Brazil), see Magnus Mörner, "Labor Systems and Patterns of Social Stratification in Colonial America: North and South," in Wolfgang Reinhard and Peter Waldmann, eds., *Nord und Süd in Amerika*, I (Freiburg: Rombach, 1992), pp. 347-362.

124 Alexander von Humboldt examined this system of "castas" in 1800; see his magnificent sociology of Mexico: *Essai politique sur le royaume de la Nouvelle-Espagne*, 2nd ed., I (Paris: Renouard, 1825), pp. 451-467.

125 To combine ethnic and socioeconomic class criteria, some researchers now use the concept of "social race." See John E. Kicza, "The Social and Ethnic Historiography of Colonial Latin America: The Last Twenty Years," in *William and Mary Quarterly*, 45 (1988), pp. 468 f.

126 This is the thesis of Colin M. MacLachlan and Jaime E. Rodriguez O., *The Forging of the Cosmic Race: A Reinterpretation of Colonial Mexico* (Berkeley: Univ. of California Press, 1980).

127 Herbert S. Klein compares the individual colonies in *African Slavery in Latin America and the Caribbean* (New York: Oxford Univ. Press, 1986), pp. 217-241.

128 Franklin W. Knight, *The Caribbean: The Genesis of a Fragmented Nationalism*, 2nd ed. (New York: Oxford Univ. Press, 1990), p. 179.

129 See Ronald Hyam, *Empire and Sexuality: The British Experience* (Manchester & New York: Manchester Univ. Press, 1990).

130 See Kenneth Ballhatchet, *Race, Sex, and Class under the Raj: Imperial Attitudes and Policies and Their Critics, 1793-1905* (New York: St. Martin's Press, 1980), p. 144 and passim.

131 See Richard H. Grove, "Colonial Conservation, Ecological Hegemony and Popular Resistance: Towards a Global Synthesis," in John M. MacKenzie, ed., *Imperialism and the Natural World* (Manchester & New York: Manchester Univ. Press, 1990), pp. 15-50; see also the thematic overview of Jacques Pouchepadass, "Colonisations et environnement," in *Revue française d'histoire d'outre-mer*, 81 (1993), pp. 5-22.

132 A wonderful document is Henry Yule and A. C. Burnell, eds., *Hobson-Jobson: A Glossary of Colloquial Anglo-Indian Words and Phrases* (Calcutta, 1886; rpt. New York: Routledge, 1986).

133 See C. R. Boxer, *The Portuguese Seaborne Empire 1415-1825* (London: Hutchinson, 1969), pp. 256-258.

134 See Blair B. Kling and M.N. Pearson, eds., *The Age of Partnership: Europeans in Asia before Dominion* (Honolulu: Univ. Press of Hawaii, 1979).

135 See Jörg Fisch, *Geschichte Südafrikas* (as in fn. 41), pp. 288-290.

136 See Jean Gelman Taylor, *The Social World of Batavia: European and Eurasian in Dutch Asia* (Madison: Univ. of Wisconsin Press, 1983), pp. 96

ff., esp. 102 and 113.

137   See Evelyn Abel, *The Anglo-Indian Community: Survival in India* (Delhi: Chanakya Publications, 1988), pp. 15 ff.; P. J. Marshall, "British Immigration into India in the Nineteenth Century," in P. C. Emmer & M. Mörner, eds., *European Expansion and Migration* (New York & Oxford: Berg Publishers, 1992), p. 192.

138   See John G. Butcher, *The British in Malaya 1880-1941: The Social History of a European Community in Colonial South East Asia* (Kuala Lumpur & New York: Oxford Univ. Press, 1979), pp. 80-83; Rajat Kanta Ray, *Social Conflict and Political Unrest in Bengal 1875-1927* (Delhi: Oxford Univ. Press, 1984), p. 22.

139   See the oral history statements in Zareer Masani, *Indian Tales of the Raj* (London: BBC Books, 1987), pp. 51-70.

140   See A. Adu Boahen, *African Perspectives on Colonialism* (Baltimore: Johns Hopkins University Press, 1987), pp. 17-26; Imanuel Geiss, *Panafrikanismus. Zur Geschichte der Dekolonisation* (Frankfurt: Europäische Verlagsanstalt, 1968), pp. 83 ff.

141   Further data on colonial urbanization have been compiled by Paul Bairoch, *De Jéricho à Mexico: Villes et économie dans l'histoire* (Paris: Gallimard, 1985), pp. 490-546. See also the brief portraits of British colonial cities in Andrew N. Porter, ed., *Atlas of British Overseas Expansion* (London: Routledge, 1991), pp. 218-237.

142   Janet Abu-Lughod, "A Tale of Two Cities: The Origins of Modern Cairo," in *Comparative Studies in Society and History,* 7 (1965), p. 429.

143   See Anthony D. King, *Colonial Urban Development: Culture, Social Power and Environment* (London & Boston: Routledge & Paul, 1976), pp. 231-275.

144   According to David Prochaska, *Making Algeria French: Colonialism in Bône, 1870-1920* (Cambridge & New York: Cambridge Univ. Press, 1990) p. 18.

145   See Susan Abeyasekere, *Jakarta: A History* (Singapore & New York: Oxford Univ. Press, 1989), pp. 60-67; Teo Siew-eng & Victor B. Savage, "Singapore Landscape: A Historical Overview of Housing Image," in Ernest C. T. Chew and Edwin Lee, eds., *A History of Singapore* (Singapore and New York: Oxford Univ. Press, 1991), pp. 314-317 (quotation on p. 317).

146   See Gérard Leclerc, *Anthropologie et colonialisme* (Paris: Librairie Arthème Fayard, 1972), pp. 113-124.

147   J. S. Furnivall, *Netherlands India: A Study of a Plural Economy* (Cambridge: Cambridge Univ. Press, 1944), p. 446. See also J. S. Furnivall, *Colonial Policy and Practice* (as in fn. 25), pp. 303-312.

148   See M. G. Smith, *The Plural Society in the British West Indies* (Berkeley:

Univ. of California Press, 1965), esp. pp. 66-74.

149 Furnivall, *Colonial Policy and Practice* (as in fn. 25), p. 306.

150 See Donald L. Horowitz, *Ethnic Groups in Conflict* (Berkeley: Univ. of California Press, 1985), pp. 135-139.

151 V. S. Naipaul, *The Overcrowded Barracoon and Other Articles* (London: Deutsch, 1972), p. 37.

152 Nathan Wachtel, *The Vision of the Vanquished: The Spanish Conquest of Peru through Indian Eyes, 1530-1570* (New York: Barnes & Noble, 1977), p. 85.

153 See Denys Lombard, *Le carrefour javanais: Essai d'histoire globale*, I (Paris: Editions de l'Ecole des hautes études en sciences sociales, 1990), pp. 79-81.

154 See John L. Phelan, *The Hispanization of the Philippines: Spanish Aims and Filipino Responses, 1565-1700* (Madison: Univ. of Wisconsin Press, 1959).

155 See Horst Gründer, *Welteroberung und Christentum. Ein Handbuch zur Geschichte der Neuzeit* (Gütersloh: Gütersloher Verlagshaus G. Mohn, 1992), pp. 315 ff.

156 An important study on this theme beyond the specific case it treats is Holger Bernt Hansen, *Mission, Church and State in a Colonial Setting: Uganda 1890-1925* (New York: St. Martin's Press, 1984), pp. 456 ff.

157 Reinhard, *Geschichte der europäischen Expansion* (as in fn. 22), IV, 204 f.

158 Alexander von Humboldt, *Lateinamerika am Vorabend der Unabhängigkeitsrevolution. Eine Anthologie von Impressionen und Urteilen*, compiled from his travel diaries and annotated by Margot Faak (Berlin: Akademie-Verlag, 1982), p. 143.

159 For a fascinating discussion of this issue, see Serge Gruzinski, *The Conquest of Mexico: The Incorporation of Indian Societies into the Western World, 16th-18th Centuries* (Cambridge: Polity Press, 1993).

160 Heinrich von Stientencron, in Hans Küng and Heinrich von Stientencron, *Christentum und Weltreligionen: Hinduismus*, 2nd ed. (Gütersloh: Gerd Mohn, 1991), p. 26. See also Vasudha Dalmia and Heinrich von Stietencron, eds., *Representing Hinduism: The Construction of Religious Traditions and National Identity* (New Delhi: Sage, 1995). On the fluidity of religious forms in India, see the major study by Susan Bayly, *Saints, Goddesses and Kings: Muslims and Christians in South Indian Society 1700-1900* (Cambridge and New York: Cambridge Univ. Press, 1990), p. 71 and passim.

161 See Dietmar Rothermund, "Nationalismus und sozialer Wandel in der Dritten Welt: Zwölf Thesen," in Otto Dann, ed., *Nationalismus und sozialer Wandel* (Hamburg: Hoffmann und Campe, 1978), p. 193 f., 195 f.

162 See J. M. Gullick, *Malay Society in the Late Nineteenth Century: The*

Beginnings of Change (Singapore & New York: Oxford Univ. Press, 1987), p. 296; Michael G. Peletz, *A Share of the Harvest: Kinship, Property, and Social History among the Malays of Rembau* (Berkeley: Univ. of California Press, 1988), p. 93.

163 Most general overviews of colonial history treat the educational system only cursorily. An exception should be noted: Denise Bouche, *Histoire de la colonisation française*, II (Paris: Fayard, 1991), pp. 243-273.

164 M. C. Ricklefs, *A History of Modern Indonesia, c. 1300 to the Present* (Bloomington: University of Indiana Press, 1981), p. 152.

165 See Christel Adick, *Die Universalisierung der modernen Schule. Eine theoretische Problemskizze zur Erklärung der weltweiten Verbreitung der modernen Schule in den letzten 200 Jahren mit Fallstudien aus Westafrika* (Paderborn: Schöningh, 1992), pp. 181 ff.

166 See Reinhard Wendt, "Sprachenvielfalt und Nationalsprache auf den Philippinen während Kolonialzeit und Unabhängigkeit," in Dagmar Hellmann-Rajanayagam and Dietmar Rothermund, eds., *Nationalstaat und Sprachkonflikte in Süd- und Südostasien* (Stuttgart: F. Steiner, 1992), p. 201.

167 See David G. Marr, *Vietnamese Tradition on Trial, 1920-1945* (Berkeley: Univ. of California Press, 1981), pp. 137 f.

168 Salman Rushdie, "'Commonwealth Literature' Does Not Exist," in Salman Rushdie, *Imaginary Homelands: Essays and Criticism 1981-1991* (London, Granta Books, 1992), p. 65.

169 Rushdie, p. 64.

170 See James Muldoon, *The Americas in the Spanish World Order: The Justification for Conquest in the Seventeenth Century* (Philadelphia: Univ. of Pennsylvania Press, 1994).

171 There is already an enormous literature on these subjects. An interesting general study is David Spurr, *The Rhetoric of Empire: Colonial Discourse in Journalism, Travel Writing, and Imperial Administration* (Durham: Duke Univ. Press, 1993). A broad range of work is sampled in Bill Ashcroft, Gareth Griffiths and Helen Tiffin, eds., *The Post-Colonial Studies Reader* (New York: Routledge, 1995).

172 See Albert Memmi, *The Colonizer and the Colonized*, introd. Jean-Paul Sartre (Boston: Beacon Press, 1991), pp. 19-44.

173 Aimé Césaire's *Discours sur le colonialisme* (Paris: Réclamé) and Oscar Mannoni's *Psychologie de la colonisation* (Paris: Editions du Seuil), two key texts of anticolonialism, both appeared in 1950.

174 Quoted in Michael Banton, *Racial Theories* (Cambridge & New York: Cambridge Univ. Press, 1987), p. vii.

175 See also Robert Ross, "Reflections on a Theme" in Robert Ross, ed., *Racism and Colonialism* (The Hague: M. Nijhoff Publishers for the Leiden

Univ. Press, 1982), pp.7 f.

176 For a study of Southeast Asia, see Syed Hussein Alatas, *The Myth of the Lazy Native* (London: Frank Cass, 1977), esp. pp. 112 ff.

177 Edward Said, *Orientalism* (New York: Random House, 1979).

178 See Raoul Girardet, *L'idée coloniale en France de 1871 à 1962* (Paris: Pluriel, 1979), pp. 136-138.

179 On the paranoid mentality of settler minorities, see the brilliant study by Dane Kennedy, *Isles of White* (as in fn. 72), pp. 128-148.

180 Johannes Fabian, *Language and Colonial Power: The Appropriation of Swahili in the Former Belgian Congo, 1880-1938* (Cambridge & New York: Cambridge Univ. Press, 1986), p. 24.

181 P. J. Vatikiotis, *The History of Egypt: From Muhammad Ali to Mubarak*, 3rd ed. (Baltimore: Johns Hopkins Univ. Press, 1986), p. 173. See also Timothy Mitchell, *Colonising Egypt* (Cambridge & New York: Cambridge Univ. Press, 1988), pp. 154-160, as well as the general overview by A. P. Thornton, *Imperialism in the Twentieth Century* (Minneapolis: Univ. of Minnesota Press, 1977), pp. 38-70.

182 Nirad C. Chaudhuri, *Thy Hand, Great Anarch! India: 1921-1952* (London: Chatto and Windus, 1987), p. 13.

183 See Judith E. Walsh, *Growing Up in British India: Indian Autobiographers on Childhood and Education under the Raj* (New York: Holmes & Meier, 1983), pp. 60 f.

184 On the state of research in this area, see Jürgen Osterhammel, "Spätkolonialismus und Dekolonisation," in *Neue Politische Literatur,* 37 (1992), pp. 404-424.

185 Nikolaus Werz provides an overview in *Das neuere politische und sozialwissenschaftliche Denken in Lateinamerika* (Freiburg: Arnold-Bergstraesser-Institut, 1991), chs. 4 and 6.

186 See Heinz Gollwitzer, *Geschichte des weltpolitischen Denkens*, II (Göttingen: Vandenhoeck & Ruprecht, 1982), pp. 322-337, 575-626; Bassam Tibi, "Politische Ideen in der 'Dritten Welt' während der Dekolonisation," in Iring Fetscher and Herfried Münkler, eds., *Pipers Handbuch der politischen Ideen*, V (Munich: Piper, 1987), pp. 361-402.

187 The three phases of decolonization were discussed in chapter III ("Colonial Epochs").

188 See Guy Pervillé, *De l'Empire français à la décolonisation* (Paris: Hachette, 1991); Raymond F. Betts, *France and Decolonisation 1900-1960* (London: Macmillan, 1991).

189 See John Darwin, *Britain and Decolonisation: The Retreat from Empire in the Post-War World* (Basingstoke: Macmillan, 1988); John Darwin, *The End of the British Empire: The Historical Debate* (Cambridge, MA: B. Blackwell, 1991); A. N. Porter and A. J. Stockwell, *British Imperial Policy*

and Decolonization 1938-64, 2 vols. (Basingstoke: Macmillan, 1987-1989).

190 See David Reynolds, *Britannia Overruled: British Policy and World Power in the Twentieth Century* (London & New York: Longman, 1991), pp. 226-234.

191 See Gervase Clarence-Smith, *The Third Portuguese Empire, 1825-1975: A Study in Economic Imperialism* (Manchester: Manchester Univ. Press, 1985), pp. 192 ff.

192 See Paul Gordon Lauren, *Power and Prejudice: The Politics and Diplomacy of Racial Discrimination* (Boulder: Westview Press, 1988).

193 See Miles Kahler, *Decolonization in Britain and France: The Domestic Consequences of International Relations* (Princeton: Princeton Univ. Press, 1984).

194 See Charles-Robert Agéron, *La décolonisation française* (Paris: A. Colin, 1991), pp. 160 f.

195 On the internal structure of the Russian/Soviet empire, see the masterful study of Andreas Kappeler, *Ru§land als Vielvölkerreich. Entstehung, Geschichte, Zerfall* (Munich: Beck, 1992); see also Dominic Lieven, "The Russian Empire and the Soviet Union as Imperial Polities," in *Journal of Contemporary History,* 30 (1995), pp. 607-636.

196 For historical background on this issue, see Sabine Dabringhaus, "Machtkämpfe auf dem Dach der Welt. Tibet zwischen chinesischem und britischem Imperialismus," in Jürgen Osterhammel, *Asien in der Neuzeit. Sieben historische Stationen* (Frankfurt: Fischer, 1994), pp. 65-81.

197 See John G. Taylor, *Indonesia's Forgotten War: The Hidden History of East Timor* (London: Zed Books, 1991).

198 See Emma Playfair, ed., *International Law and the Administration of Occupied Territories: Two Decades of Israeli Occupation of the West Bank and Gaza Strip* (New York: Oxford Univ. Press, 1992).

199 See Gerald Segal, *The Fate of Hong Kong* (New York: St. Martin's Press, 1993). On other British possessions, see George Drower, *Britain's Dependent Territories: A Fistful of Islands* (Brookfield, VT: Dartmouth, 1992).

200 Robert Aldrich and John Connell, *France's Overseas Frontier: Départements et territoires d'outre-mer* (Cambridge & New York: Cambridge Univ. Press, 1992), p. 245.

Selected Readings

A. General

Albertini, Rudolf von. *European Colonial Rule, 1880-1940: The Impact of the West on India, Southeast Asia, and Africa.* Oxford: Clio Press, 1982.

Berque, Jacques. *French North Africa.* London: Faber, 1967.

Betts, Raymond F. *The False Dawn: European Imperialism in the Nineteenth Century.* Minneapolis: Univ. of Minnesota Press, 1976.

————. *Uncertain Dimensions. Western Overseas Empires in the Twentieth Century.* Oxford: Oxford Univ. Press, 1985.

Curtin, Philip D. *The Rise and Fall of the Plantation Complex. Essays in Atlantic History.* Cambridge: Cambridge Univ. Press, 1990.

Dirks, Nicholas B., ed. *Colonialism and Culture.* Ann Arbor: Univ. of Michigan Press, 1992.

Doyle, Michael W. *Empires,* Ithaca: Cornell Univ. Press, 1986.

Fieldhouse, David K. *Colonialism 1870-1945. An Introduction.* London: Macmillan, 1981.

Fisch, Jörg. *Die europäische Expansion und das Völkerrecht. Die Auseinandersetzungen um den Status der überseeischen Gebiete vom 15. Jahrhundert bis zur Gegenwart.* Stuttgart: Franz Steiner, 1984.

Guillaume, Pierre. *Le monde coloniale, XIX-XXe siècle,* 2nd ed. Paris: Armand Colin, 1994.

Gründer, Horst. *Welteroberung und Christentum. Ein Handbuch zur Geschichte der Neuzeit.* Gütersloh: Mohn, 1992.

Hobsbawm, Eric. *The Age of Empire, 1875-1914.* London: Weidenfeld & Nicolson, 1987.

Holland, Robert F. *European Decolonization 1918-1981.* Basingstoke & London: Macmillan, 1985.

Kiernan, Victor G. *The Lords of Human Kind. European Attitudes to the Outside World in the Imperial Age.* Harmondsworth: Penguin, 1972.

————. *European Empires from Conquest to Collapse, 1815-1960.* London: Fontana, 1982.

Low, D.A. *The Egalitarian Moment: Asia and Africa, 1950-1980.* Cambridge: Cambridge Univ. Press, 1996.

Miège, Jean-Louis. *Expansion européenne et décolonisation de 1870 à nos jours,* 2nd ed. Paris: Presses Universitaires Français, 1986.

Mommsen, Wolfgang J. *Theories of Imperialism.* Chicago: Univ. of Chicago Press, 1982.

Mommsen, Wolfgang J. and Jürgen Osterhammel, eds. *Imperialism and After. Continuities and Discontinuities.* London: Allen & Unwin, 1986.

Olson, James S., ed. *Historical Dictionary of European Imperialism*. New York & Westport, CN.: Greenwood Press, 1991.

Parry, John H. *The Age of Reconnaissance: Discovery, Exploration and Settlement, 1450-1650*. London: Weidenfeld & Nicolson, 1963.

———. *Trade and Dominion: European Overseas Empires in the Eighteenth Century*. London: Weidenfeld & Nicolson, 1971.

Porter, Andrew N. *European Imperialism, 1860-1914*. Basingstoke & London: Macmillan, 1994.

Prakash, Gyan, ed. *After Colonialism: Imperial Histories and Postcolonial Displacements*. Princeton: Princeton Univ. Press, 1995.

Reinhard, Wolfgang. *Geschichte der europäischen Expansion*, 4 vols., Stuttgart: Kohlhammer, 1983-1990.

———. *Kleine Geschichte des Kolonialismus*. Stuttgart: Kröner, 1996.

Scammell, G.V. *The World Encompassed: The First European Maritime Empires, c. 800-1650*. London & New York: Methuen, 1989.

Scammell, G.V., *The First Imperial Age. European Overseas Expansion c. 1400-1715*. London: Unwin Hyman, 1989.

Schmitt, Eberhard, ed. *Dokumente zur Geschichte der europäischen Expansion*. Munich: Beck, 1984ff.

Thomas, Nicholas. *Colonialism's Culture: Anthropology, Travel, and Government*. Cambridge: Polity Press, 1994.

Trotha, Trutz von. *Koloniale Herrschaft*. Tübingen: Mohr-Siebeck, 1994.

B. Individual Colonial Empires and Areas of Colonization

Aldrich, Robert. *The French Presence in the South Pacific, 1842-1940*. Basingstoke & London, 1990.

———. *Greater France: A History of French Overseas Expansion*. Basingstoke & London: Macmillan, 1996.

Allworth, Edward, ed. *Central Asia: 120 Years of Russian Rule*. Durham, NC: Duke Univ. Press, 1989.

Bayly, C.A. *Indian Society and the Making of the British Empire*. Cambridge: Cambridge Univ. Press, 1988.

———, ed., *Atlas of the British Empire*, New York: Facts on File, 1989.

———, ed. *The Raj: India and the British 1600-1947*. London: National Portrait Gallery Publications, 1990.

Beckles, Hilary and Verene Shepherd, eds. *Caribbean Slave Society and Economy: A Student Reader*. Kingston & London: Ian Randle & James Currey, 1991.

Bethell, Leslie, ed. *The Cambridge History of Latin America*, vols. 1-2. Cambridge: Cambridge Univ. Press, 1984.

Boahen, A. Adu, ed. *General History of Africa*. Volume 7: *Africa under Colonial*

Domination 1880-1935. Paris and London: Heinemann, 1985.

Bouche, Denise. *Histoire de la colonisation française.* Volume 2: *Flux et reflux, 1815-1962.* Paris: Fayard, 1991.

Boxer, C.R. *The Dutch Seaborne Empire, 1600-1800.* London: Hutchinson, 1965.

———. *The Portuguese Seaborne Empire, 1415-1825.* London: Hutchinson, 1969.

Brown, Judith M. *Modern India: The Origins of an Asian Democracy.* Delhi: Oxford Univ. Press, 1985.

Brunschwig, Henri. *French Colonialism, 1871-1914: Myths and Realities.* London: Pall Mall Press, 1966.

Burkholder, Mark A. and Lyman L. Johnson. *Colonial Latin America.* New York & Oxford: Oxford Univ. Press, 1990.

Cain, P.J. and A.G. Hopkins. *British Imperialism,* 2 vols. London & New York: Longman, 1993.

Canny, Nicholas and Anthony Pagden, eds. *Colonial Identity in the Atlantic World.* Princeton: Princeton Univ. Press, 1987.

Clayton, Anthony. *The Wars of French Decolonization.* Harlow: Longman, 1994.

Cohen, William B. *Rulers of Empire: The French Colonial Service in Africa.* Stanford: Stanford Univ. Press, 1971.

Fage, J.D. and Roland Oliver, eds. *The Cambridge History of Africa.* Cambridge: Cambridge Univ. Press, vols. 6 (1985), 7 (1986), 8 (1984).

Fisch, Jörg. *Geschichte Südafrikas.* Munich: Deutscher Taschenbuch Verlag, 1990.

Forsyth, James. *A History of the Peoples of Siberia: Russia's North Asian Colony, 1581-1990.* Cambridge: Cambridge Univ. Press, 1992.

Gann, L.H. & Peter Duignan, eds. *Colonialism in Africa, 1870-1960.* 5 vols. Cambridge: Cambridge Univ. Press, 1969-1975.

———, eds. *The Rulers of British Africa 1870-1914.* London: Croom Helm, 1978.

———, eds. *The Rulers of Belgian Africa 1884-1914.* Princeton: Princeton Univ. Press, 1979.

Gifford, Prosser and William Roger Louis, eds. *The Transfer of Power in Africa: Decolonization 1940-1960.* New Haven: Yale Univ. Press, 1982.

Gründer, Horst. *Geschichte der deutschen Kolonien,* 3rd ed. Paderborn: Schöningh, 1995.

Hall, D.G.E. *A History of South-East Asia,* 4th ed. Basingstoke & London: Macmillan, 1981.

Iliffe, John. *Africa: The History of a Continent.* Cambridge: Cambridge Univ. Press, 1995.

James, Lawrence. *The Rise and Fall of the British Empire.* Boston: Little, Brown, 1994.

Judd, Denis. *Empire: The British Imperial Experience from 1765 to the Present.* New York: HarperCollins, 1996.

Kappeler, Andreas. *Ruβland als Vielvölkerreich. Entstehung, Geschichte, Zerfall.* Munich: Beck, 1992.

Karnow, Stanley. *In Our Image: America's Empire in the Philippines.* New York: Ballantine Books, 1989.

Kociumbas, Jan. *The Oxford History of Australia.* Volume 2: *Colonial Australia, 1770-1860.* Melbourne: Oxford Univ. Press, 1991.

Knight, Franklin W. *The Caribbean. The Genesis of a Fragmented Nationalism.* 2nd ed. New York: Oxford Univ. Press, 1990.

Kulke, Hermann and Dietmar Rothermund. *History of India.* London: Routledge, 1990.

Kumar, Dharma, ed. *The Cambridge Economic History of India.* Volume 2: *c. 1757-c. 1970.* Cambridge: Cambridge Univ. Press, 1982.

Lewis, Gordon K. *The Growth of the Modern West Indies.* New York & London: Monthly Review Press, 1968.

Lockhart, James and Stuart B. Schwartz. *Early Latin America. A History of Colonial Spanish America and Brazil.* Cambridge: Cambridge Univ. Press, 1983.

Low, D.A. *Eclipse of Empire.* Cambridge: Cambridge Univ. Press, 1991.

McAlister, Lyle N. *Spain and Portugal in the New World 1492-1700.* Minneapolis: Univ. of Minnesota Press, 1984.

McFarlane, Anthony. *The British in the Americas, 1480-1815.* Harlow: Longman, 1994.

Manning, Patrick. *Francophone Sub-Saharan Africa 1880-1985.* Cambridge: Cambridge Univ. Press, 1988.

Marseille, Jacques. *Empire colonial et capitalisme français: Histoire d'un divorce.* Paris: Albin Michel, 1984.

Marshall, P.J., ed. *The Cambridge Illustrated History of the British Empire.* Cambridge: Cambridge Univ. Press, 1996.

Meyer, Jean et al. *Histoire de la France coloniale.* Volume 1: *Des origines à 1914.* Paris: Armand Colin, 1991.

Middleton, Richard. *Colonial America. A History.* Cambridge, Mass. & Oxford: Blackwell, 1992.

Miège, Jean-Louis. *L'imperialisme colonial italien de 1870 à nos jours.* Paris: Presses Universitaires de France, 1968.

Myers, Ramon H. and Mark R. Peattie, eds. *The Japanese Colonial Empire, 1895-1945.* Princeton: Princeton Univ. Press, 1984.

Navarro Garc'a, Luis, ed. *Historia de las Américas,* 4 vols. Madrid: Alhambra Longman, 1991.

Oliver, W.H., ed. *The Oxford History of New Zealand.* Oxford: Clarendon Press, 1981.

Osterhammel, Jürgen. *China und die Weltgesellschaft. Vom 18. Jahrhundert bis in unsere Zeit.* Munich: Beck, 1989.

————, ed. *Asien in der Neuzeit 1500-1950. Sieben historische Stationen.* Frankfurt: Fischer, 1994.

Peattie, Mark R. "The Japanese Colonial Empire, 1895-1945." In: Peter Duus, ed., *The Cambridge History of Japan.* Volume 6: *The Twenthieth Century.* Cambridge: Cambridge Univ. Press, 1988, pp. 217-270.

Porter, Andrew N., ed. *Atlas of British Overseas Expansion.* London: Routledge, 1991.

Rothermund, Dietmar. *An Economic History of India: From Pre-Colonial Times to 1986.* London, New York & Sydney: Croom Helm, 1988.

Ruedy, John. *Modern Algeria: The Origins and Development of a Nation.* Bloomington & Indianapolis: Indiana Univ. Press, 1992.

Sarkar, Sumit. *Modern India, 1885-1947*, 2nd ed. Basingstoke & London: Macmillan, 1989.

Scarr, Deryck. *The History of the Pacific Islands: Kingdoms of the Reefs.* Melbourne: Macmillan, 1990.

Schirmer, Daniel B. & Steven R. Shalom. *The Philippines Reader: A History of Colonialism, Neocolonialism, Dictatorship, and Resistance.* Boston: South End Press, 1987.

Smith, Woodruff D. *The German Colonial Empire.* Chapel Hill: Univ. of North Carolina Press, 1978.

Subrahmanyam, Sanjay. *The Portuguese Empire in Asia, 1500-1700: A Political and Economic History.* Harlow: Longman, 1993.

Tarling, Nicholas, ed. *The Cambridge History of Southeast Asia,* 2 vols. Cambridge: Cambridge Univ. Press, 1992.

Thobie, Jacques et al. *Histoire de la France coloniale.* Volume 2: *1914-1990.* Paris: Armand Colin, 1990.

Thompson, Leonard. *A History of South Africa.* New Haven: Yale Univ. Press, 1992.

Tignor, Robert L. *Modernisation and British Colonial Rule in Egypt.* Princeton: Princeton Univ. Press, 1966.

Tomlinson, B.R. *The Economy of Modern India, 1860-1970.* Cambridge: Cambridge Univ. Press, 1993.

Van Goor, J. *De Nederlandse Koloni'n. Geschiedenis van de Nederlandse expansie 1600-1975.* The Hague: SDU Uitgeverij, 1994.

Watts, David. *The West Indies: Patterns of Development, Culture and Environmental Change since 1492.* Cambridge: Cambridge Univ. Press, 1987.

Wilson, Henry S. *African Decolonization.* London: Edward Arnold, 1994.

Index